11-20-68

The
Torture
of
Mothers

The Torture of Mothers

by Truman Nelson

Introduction by Maxwell Geismar

BEACON PRESS · BOSTON

To Conrad J. Lynn

THE LAST OF THE GREAT ABOLITIONISTS

Photographs by Peter Lenz

PUBLISHER'S NOTE

Truman Nelson wrote *The Torture of Mothers* in the Autumn of 1964 in the aftermath of Harlem's "long hot summer." The bulk of the book consists of tapes taken directly from the lips of mothers and children, the victims of the incidents he describes here. Despite considerable searching he was unable to find a commercial publisher who would take the book and decided to publish it on his own Garrison Press. Since then the book has made the rounds in a kind of private literary circuit but has received almost no attention from the major reviews. *Ramparts* published a short selection from this powerful book in July 1966 and the Beacon edition is published with the hope that the book will now attract the concern which it deserves.

CHAPTER ONE

How can I make you believe this? This is what is blocking the long outcry in my throat, impacting the anger and frustration until I too become dumb and sick with the gorge and glut of my own indigestible fury. Even keeping my voice down, even speaking to you in a whisper, my breath staggers and halts under the weight of this monstrous wrong.

Perhaps if I said the victims were guilty, in some small way, I could get you to suspend your disbelief. Perhaps I could get you in that region where all humanity can merge in a common sadness over human hurt . . . there beyond all the rules of innocence and guilt that man has made. Very well, three boys, all black, and two men, one black and one white, did interfere, or did interpose, in a questioning or resistant way between the police and some supposed wrong-doers.

It is important to know that this happened in Harlem and was, therefore, a *racial* incident. Our sensibilities act differently when that word comes into play. White teen-agers, college boys on a spring rampage, on panty raids, beach sleep-outs have now made an American tradition out of assaulting police, turning police cars over and setting fire to them. When we read about this we settle back with an indulgent shrug and dismiss it from our minds. One scarcely bothers to read what the punishment was for these acts against the state . . . we know in advance that it will be light and easy, a mere admonishment.

But when it concerns black against white, when it is racial, we cannot see the fun in it. It frightens us. We suddenly see the snarl on the tiger at the other end of the tail these same police are holding for us. We tell ourselves hastily we do not want the black people of

Harlem to be slaves . . . but we do like them to be a little servile. After all, we are all a little servile to the police. Of course, we want the black men in Harlem to be servile and stand quietly by while their brothers and sisters, their children, are being beaten.

Somehow, we do not really believe this is happening. How could we, in God's name, *know* that this happens and expect these citizens and men to stand by without interceding by word or gesture while little kids not yet in high school are kicked and cuffed and beaten over their heads with clubs until they are bleeding? We do not see this, we do not hear this, because if we did, we too would bleed, because when a man has a conscience, and it is real, and active, and free, then it bleeds in times like this. Sorry . . . I am starting to raise my voice.

The incident, now known as the Harlem Fruit Riot, is described in the New York *Times* from the retrospective date of May 29, like this:[1]

> On April 17, about 75 Negro children on their way home from school overturned some cartons at a Harlem fruit and vegetable stand, and what might have been a minor incident grew into a riot.

On April 19, the *Times* carried this story slightly different:[2]

> The defendants, four youths and a man, were involved in a free-for-all on Friday afternoon, after they allegedly overturned a fruit stand at 368 Lenox Avenue, near 128th Street.

The difference in the two stories is important. The May 29th story is the police version which never fails to disfigure the most simple occurrence with errors of fact, nor to compress within the tiniest compass of its utterance some form of malignancy. The truth was that there were three boys and two men. The men, Fecundo Acion, a Puerto Rican seaman forty-seven years old, and Frank Stafford, a salesman, had no conceivable reason for overturning a fruit stand and pelting the proprietor with fruit, as they were charged with doing. The three boys, Wallace Baker, nineteen, Daniel Hamm, eighteen, and Frederick Frazier, sixteen, were definitely cleared by the proprietor, who told the police they were not at his store.

The police say the five they arrested made the incident into a riot. The five they arrested say the police made it into a riot. The case has just come to trial in the courts. We are still left with the explanation of the arrested five, who charge the police with gross brutality. The police denied the charge but refused to elaborate. "We will not dignify the charges," one official explained. But the defendants tell their stories with a passion that confers a dignity on them beyond the power of the police to dismiss stories that do not all fit together like links in a chain but are more like rays of flashing, searing light, illuminating a landscape of pain.

First Frank Stafford: an American prototype, thirty-one years old, a family man with two kids and a nonworking wife, plays a good game of basketball on Sunday; a salesman, hits the sidewalks of Harlem with a neat attache case and a peddlers license; goes in and out of houses, stores, beauty parlors, offering ladies' hosiery, mens' socks and shorts, flowers in the springtime, horns and favors at New Year's time, anything to decently support his family . . . an American prototype, except that he's black.

April 17, in the afternoon, he came out of 110 129th Street. Mrs. Evelyn Johnson had wanted to buy some of his stockings, but he didn't have her size and he told her he'd be back on Monday if she'd wait. She said she would if he'd be sure to bring back the exact shade she had picked out. Frank was going to call on another customer at 166 129th, and then go to the Jolly Day Store. He had nine boxes of stockings in the case he was carrying in his hand. When he got to the street he saw many people, many police, little boys running. In the windows people were standing and staring out. But there were more police in the street than there were people in the windows. And the police had their guns out and the people on the sidewalk were shouting, "they got their guns out, they got their guns out." And the people in the windows drew back for fear of getting shot at. The police were pointing their guns at the roofs. Frank got down two houses beyond Evelyn Johnson's and then his life abruptly changed.[3]

FRANK STAFFORD

They had this kid in between the cops.
So I spoke up and asked them, Why are you beating
    him like that?
You all going to take him on to jail.
    you don't have to beat him like that.
Police jump up and start swinging on me.
He put the gun on me and said get over there.
I said what for?
Then one hit me on the back of the head from
    behind.
I tried to protect myself,
Moving in towards the one that was in front of me.
I tried to fight, but it wasn't useful, because there
    was three of them.
I was in the Series, I was in the midst of three
    policemen.
Then one hit me on my right shoulder,
And when I turned to my left there was a cross blow,
You know, a swing crossways.
He hit me up side of my eye.
Then all the pain like a crack ran through my
    whole head.
The best thing I could do then was fold up
And try to protect myself on the ground.
I fell on the ground trying to protect my lower parts
So they wouldn't hit me or kick me there.
But my eye was hurting so from the pain I kept
    moving my hand on it.
One police he took and stepped on my thumb to
    hold my hand behind me.

4

On my thumb now, the bone is kind of out of shape.

The other one he brought my other hand around
and put the cuffs on.

I felt my eye was out.

Even this lady on the street she told me.

She told me, she say Frank, go along with them,
go along with them,

'Cause your eye is all messed up.

The police see my eye in the street, I mean the
condition of it.

They didn't say anything, all they did was holler
let's go, let's go.

They snatched me up and partially dragged me to
the detective car.

There was another young kid in there.

They took me upstairs in the detective office and
there they started,

Like when everyone else got there, they started
beating on us.

They came in with oranges and started smashing
them in people's faces,

Saying . . . you like fruit, you like oranges, well
try these.

There were five of us, all handcuffed behind our
backs.

It went on for a while. About thirty-five I'd say

Came into the room and started beating, punching
us in the jaw,

In the stomach, in the chest, beating us with a
padded club . . .

It's not a blackjack but it's got leather on it

And it's got big stitches on the side and it's about
twelve inches long.

They just beat us across the back, pull us on the
floor,

Spit on us, call us niggers, dogs, animals.

You got what you deserve, these are the things that
they said to us.

They call us dogs and animals when I don't see why.

We are the dogs and animals the way they are
    beating us.
They called us cop-fighters, that was the name
    that they used,
Cop-fighters.
And every cop that come in they holler, oh you are
    the cop-fighters
And punch me in the chest, in the jaw, in the
    stomach.
When they first start beating us they rest up for a
    little while,
Like went out and rested and started all over again.
I can't describe any of them becuse the only way
    you can describe a police is by his badge.
They took off their coats and put on their sweat
    sweaters and come in
Like they were going to a gymnasium or something
    to have a sparring match.
There was this old man they were beating back in
    the street,
He said his age was forty-seven years old when we
    got into the station,
Like they beat me they beat the other kids and
    the elderly fellow.
They throw him almost through one of the radiators.
Two of them pick him up and throw him into the
    wall.
I thought he was dead over there.
And being I wouldn't fall on the floor,
They grabbed me and pulled a little piece out of
    my neck.
I still have the scratch.
And all the time we were handcuffed behind our
    backs.
They beat us up in this room a good while and an
    aide came from Harlem Hospital.
He said to me why had they called him in 'cause
    there was nothing he could do.
He put a bandage 'cross my eye.

And then they started beating us again.

But the pains I suffered I couldn't suffer no more
'cause I was already hurt.

And when they started beating on me the second
time

I was telling them they might as well kill me.

After about three or four hours they took us out
into the patrol car and took us over to Harlem
Hospital.

They said to wash up before we went.

I axed what was the percentage in that if I was
going to the hospital?

So one police said you might not get there.

Over in Harlem Hospital they say

They don't know why they brought me in.

They said there's nothing they could do for me
there

Because I needed eye surgery.

I can't say exactly what time it was, but it was
rather late.

They took me on down to Bellevue.

The doctor down there say to me you must be in
good shape

To take the whipping that I took and not have
pains down there.

They started giving me needles and stuff to knock
me out,

So they could start operating.

They operated on the eye trying to save it.

But he say that night he thought it was impossible

Because it was almost 19 hours since I took the blow.

He thought it was impossible but he was going to
try it.

So they laid me down there for about fourteen days
behind this,

Trying to save my eye.

And on the fourteenth day he told me he couldn't
wait no longer

Because it might cause infection in the other eye.

On May the second I had a second operation to
    remove the eye
So that it wouldn't strain in my right eye.
He told me all I had to do now was to be careful
And don't get no infection.
If I feel any kind of pain to come right down there
And they'd do something about my other eye.
There could have been an easier way for the police
To subdue everybody out there that day
Than going through the things we went through,
Beatings and throwing down and kicking and
    everything.
No one out there had any weapons;
The only ones that had weapons was the police.
They could have used other methods stopping what
    was going on.
But the police don't have no like for us, black
    people in general.
The way they handle this, that proved they don't
    have no like for us,
No respect.
The way they did this, really they didn't have to
    do it like this.
They was like more or less afraid.
I don't know why they should be afraid of anyone
    out there.
They have everything on their side.
They come in a drove with clubs, guns and
    everything else.
No one else out there has no weapons.
Now I just hope to get more stockings for the street
If the police don't try to take them away from me.
They might, you know. I think they know me.
Like the police department get the word around
    saying
He might be wearing a patch.
I think I'm the only fellow on the street wearing
    an eye patch right now.
I have quite a few police look at me now pretty hard.

But I don't have nothing to say. I keeping walking
    down the street
Like I don't even see them.
My lawyer he axe me to keep somebody with me at
    all times,
'Cause the police may try to mess with me again.

Frank Stafford said this into a tape recorder. His voice is pleasant, almost caressing. Its deep timbre blurs the words softly; there is no agony apparent there. There is bewilderment, mostly at the three criminal charges against him he still has to face. He was charged with beating up a schoolteacher on the corner of 127th and Lenox Avenue, and upsetting the fruit stand between 128th and 129th on Lenox Avenue, and assaulting the police on 129th Street between Seventh and Lenox Avenues, simultaneously.

But Frank was only a by-product of this nightmare. When he fell, eyeless in Harlem, his trajectory of pain had reached its zenith. There were others, two young lads who were hurled by the fruit riot into the shadow of the electric chair and to be innocent parties in the torture of their mothers . . . Wallace Baker, for example.'

WALLACE BAKER

I seen some little boys picking up fruit from the
    ground,
So they start coming toward One-Twenty-ninth and
    Lenox Avenue.
So I seen three policemen running over there
And grab one between his legs
And get ready to hit him with a stick.
So I ran over and tried to stop him.
And two of them jumped on me and beat me for
    nothing.
Then they put me in the car, handcuffed to Danny
    Hamm.
In the car they were beating the brother
For having his hand on the door,
Hitting him on the hand with the blackjack.

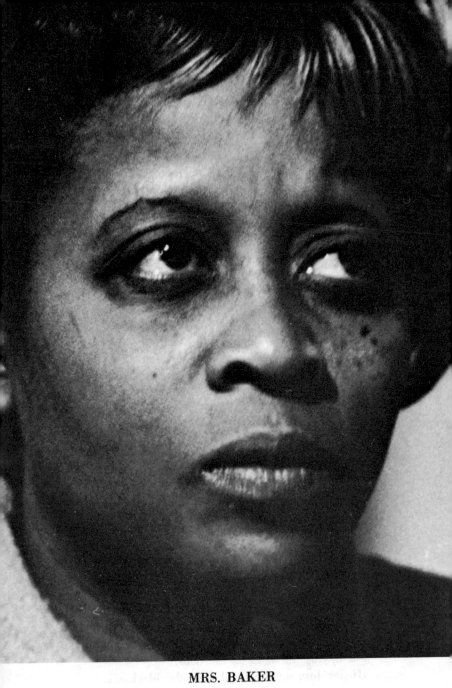

MRS. BAKER

And when they got us to the precinct station,
They beat us practically all that day,
And then at night they took us to Harlem Hospital
to get X-rays.

There is clearly a sort of guilt here; Wallace Baker
did come between the officer and the boy he was whipping. The torture of his mother began with a phone call.[5]

MRS. BAKER

And then they had the nerve to call me to come to
the hospital
To sign for Wally because they thought they had
broke his neck.
So I had to go to the hospital to sign for X-rays for
Wallace.
His neck was over one-sided.
He had a patch right across his lip, his face was
swollen.
I went in and I asked the colored cop there could
I see him?
He said yes, go in.
The white one told me to get out . . . I couldn't talk
to him.
I was wondering where Wallace was,
And a friend of mine came around and told me
they had beat Wallace
And thrown him in the police car.
I was cleaning my house, and when I finished
cleaning
I was going to the precinct.
But before I could I got a phone call, come to the
hospital.
Before they could give the X-ray, I had to sign for
it.
Danny Hamm was with Wallace, I saw him.
They had beaten him, his face was swollen.
He had a patch on his face
But his legs had knots . . .
They just took the stick and they beat him

And then they kicked him and his leg was swollen
with blood clots.
They all had blood clots on their legs.
When he got home Wallace told me
They're beating us all night ... every shift go off
and one come on.
Oh God!
How they step on their hands ... handcuffs behind
their backs.
People won't believe it.
But I could just look at him and tell practically
all what happen to him.
He still has the blood clots on his legs
They never tell me the charges on him.
I don't know what it was.
How could he know for what reason
If one group go off and another group walk in
And they say what did he do?
And then they start beating on him, took turns
beating on them,
And they continued all night ...
Call them dirty dogs, black dogs,
Everything they called them.
For them to beat them like that.
Even one of them had the nerve to spit in Wallace's
face.
How could he know why?
One set would go off, another come on . . .
All of them had to get . . . you know, this thing
out of their heads.
Wallace said after they brought them from the
hospital,
They handcuffed them all and beat them all again,
all night.
He got under the bench . . . they have those long
benches down there,
So he just rolled under the bench and pretended
he fainted.
That's what stopped them, you know.

They don't have to have a reason,
And I don't think there's nothing you could do.
They is the law and the law is always right.
You can stand up and they can shoot you down.
They in the right and you in the wrong.
Wallace and Danny were just passing at the time,
You know, that the cops were beating these kids.
Wallace said that while the police were beating the
    smaller kids
He walked up where they were beating them and
    kicking them around,
They don't have to have no reason.
And he want to know what the little kids do
So that's where they started in on him.
He didn't know the kids. He just saw the cops.
But the cops are always right . . .
They can beat whether it's a baby or not.
When that judge saw Wallace and Danny
He knew they were beaten.
Frank had one eye, he was in the hospital,
He couldn't even come to court that Saturday
    morning,
He was in the hospital.
They don't have to have no reason.

DANIEL HAMM[6]

We got halfway up the block and we heard a police
    siren,
And we didn't pay much attention to it and then
    we heard children scream.
We turned around and walked back to see what
    happened.
As I got closer to the corner I saw this policeman
    with his gun out
Waving it at some young children and with his billy
    in his hand.
I like put myself in the way to keep him from
    shooting the kids,
Because first of all he was shaking like a leaf

And jumping all over the place,
And I thought he might shoot one of them.
So I stepped in his way to keep one of the kids from
getting hurt,
Trying to find out what was going on . . . and he
turned on me.
I tried to get out of his way,
But as I ran and got in the middle of the street,
A patrolman apprehended me by the neck, flipped
me over,
And put his knee on my chest.
I couldn't move or anything, and he asked me for
my hand
And I couldn't give it, because in the position he
had me
I could only give one hand.
Finally I gave him my other hand.
He handcuffed me . . . I was handcuffed in front.
He took me to the patrol car and later one of my
friends
That was with me, named Wallace, they put him
in the car too.
We went to the precinct and that's where they beat
us
For nothing at all.
They like turned shifts on us,
Like six and twelve at a time would beat us,
And this went on practically all day we were at that
station,
They beat us till I could barely walk and my back
was in pain.
My friends they did the same till they bled.
All the time they were beating us they never took
the handcuffs off.
And when they wanted to take us to the hospital
They made us go wash up.
They didn't want to take me to the hospital because
I wasn't bleeding.

I had this big bruise on my leg from them
    beating me.
I had to like open the bruise up and let some of
    the bruise blood
Come out to show them I was bleeding,
And this is the only reason they let me go to the
    hospital.
I felt that otherwise, if I hadn't shown them this,
Then I wouldn't have went to the hospital at all.
They got so tired beating us they just came in
And start spitting on us.
And we trying to duck the spit,
But they get on me, all on my face and my hands
    and my clothes.
They even bring phlegm up and spit on me,
Walk all over the top of us,
Make us get on the floor and all that crap.
We were actually treated like animals, so to say.
No policeman, no colored ones try to stop them
    from beating us.
And when we was in the precinct and they was
    putting charges on us
They said miscellaneous mischief and other charges
    we didn't understand.
And when I ask them what did it mean, they tell
    me none of your business.
You're going to jail anyway . . . why try and find
    out what you did?
And they didn't answer any questions at all.

MRS. HAMM[1]

I didn't know anything about this.
They didn't call me.
When I saw him he couldn't pull up his pants,
He had a blood clot on each leg.
But they didn't bother to call me.
I had went to the precinct to see about him
And see about the other boy, Fred Frazier,
'Cause I knew his mother was working at the time.

MRS. HAMM

And they wouldn't let me in the precinct.

They told me he would be in court nine o'clock
  tonight

And made everybody in front of the precinct go
  away.

When I was there it was lined up with policemen

Stopping people from going in.

That night when Fred Frazier's mother came home

She had to go to the hospital to sign for him,

For twelve stitches in his head.

They kept them overnight,

Then they were bailed

And charged with incitement to riot and assault.

Danny told me they beat him all night

And how they called more ones in to help.

His hands looked like they stuck pins in them.

I know it's unbelievable but it's the truth.

Because Frank, for one, had to have an operation
  on his thumb

Because he say the policeman stepped on his
  thumb with his shoe

And turned the heel of his shoe all the way around
  on his thumb.

And that's what he said, Mr. Stafford. He had to
  have an operation.

And you could see his thumb was all swollen.

He say this policeman, he deliberately stepped on
  him

And took his heel and turned it all the way around
  on his finger.

When Danny got home he didn't cry,

He just try to pull up his pants to show me the
  blood clots.

But the pants wouldn't go up only this much over
  his legs

Because his legs were swollen so bad.

In fact he had a Red Cross plaster on his back

And it was all bruised, the back and both the legs.

There's no one I could think to go to;

You just have to fight back the best way you know.
'Cause when I saw this it was unbelievable.
I mean I just couldn't believe it.
I kept asking him are you sure, are you sure,
     because . . .
Well, I saw the blood clots and the bruises,
But I just couldn't accept a police would do a thing
     like that.
I just couldn't accept it.

And so the long hot summer began, the summer of promise, the summer of final liberation. But the jailhouse beating went on just the same. Just the same as last summer and the year before, ten, twenty, thirty years before. The same as the beatings described in the pamphlets put out in the 1930's describing the same precinct, calling it the Meat Grinder. Nothing seemed to be changing, except perhaps it was worse. Now they were beating openly in the street, in the full glare of day, without pity, without shame, under the sun.

An unemployed cook named Herbert Paine was just walking though the block . . . [8]

I saw the cops running behind a couple of kids.
They snatched at one of the kids and reached and
     grabbed at another.
So the kids were trying to find out what was
     going on.
So the cops ask why they went and bothered this
     man's fruit stand.
So the kid said listen, I don't know nothing about it.
Then they start shaking the kid around, smashing
     him around.
The kid said wait a minute, listen, don't shake me
     like this.
I don't know nothing about it.
So the kid got mad and drop his books,
Then the kid try to get away from the cop.
The cop keep pulling him and smashing him around,
So he hit him a couple of times with his stick.

So the kid say wait a minute, why are you hitting
me,
So listen I'll fight you, I'll fight for my rights, he
said.
I didn't do anything.
All of a sudden here come more cops,
And the rest of the kids they are just standing
around
And the cops start smashing every kid that they see.
So the kids just put up a fight, start fighting
with their fists.
Then this boy, this particular boy, they hit him on
the head
A couple times.
And he got mad.
He start fighting and kicking the cop and hitting
with his fist.
So three cops teamed up on this particular kid and
just beat him down.
Till he couldn't take it any more.
All he could do was give in.
He couldn't throw another lick.
So they messed up his eyes . . .
They were all bloody, his nose, mouth, head.
This was a kid no older than seventeen.
I saw the kid myself,
Fighting the cop with his fist,
Trying to get away because he didn't do nothing,
he said.
So three cops jumped on him and beat him down
with a stick,
And he couldn't move.⁹
Here come the rest of the kids.
They were throwing garbage pails,
And the cops just pull out their sticks and keep
hitting, hitting,
Hitting everybody they see standing in the street
At the particular time.

> So they smashed four or five kids and put them in
>   the car.
> Now here come an old man walking out a stoop,
>   and asked one cop
> Say, listen sir, what's going on out here?
> The cop turn around and smash him a couple of
>   times in the head.
> So that were about it.

For the record, the man that owned the fruit stand
says it was not boys from that neighborhood at all. He
had been there thirty-five years and nothing like this ever
happened. He told the officers, the boys I don't recognize.
He is a businessman, he wants domestic tranquility, no
trouble. Another businessman commented at greater
length.

> In the first place, I don't have anything against a
>   person
> Running a business and using police to protect his
>   property.
> But what really hurt me to see with my own eyes
>   was when
> A policeman don't know exactly who it was that
>   did the damage
> And just runs smashing anybody.
> It could have been me.
> I just got through doing a little work for a friend
>   of mine
> And I was walking through the block and I saw the
>   police
> Just smashing anybody,
> Just smashing anybody he thought did it,
> And just smashing them around and hammering
>   them like that.
> My goodness, anybody with common sense could
>   just explain himself
> And express himself in a way to make the police
>   understand.
> 'Cause everybody's got a sense of humor . . .
> They got to have a good sense of humor to call

themselves a police.
And work for the state . . . or for the city.
And this police come and ask me, say did you have anything to do
With this fruit and vegetable stand, and I didn't.
All I would say is no sir, I'm sorry, I don't know anything about it.
He should let me go,
Let me alone,
But not come and hit me across the head, and with his stick,
Busting my nose
And eyes
And everything, when I know nothing about it.
My goodness . . . that's too much.

The talk accumulates on the tapes. It has the ring of truth. Righteous indignation starts to rise. Well-meaning social workers rouse themselves. They make pledges. They offer hopes. Everybody agrees that to beat a man down to the ground after he is handcuffed is unmerciful. There's no reason to handle a man like that after he is handcuffed, that's for sure. *You've got a man handcuffed, there's nothing more to do than carry him off.* They want the whole world to hear these tapes. A meeting is held at Friendship Baptist Community Center, on 130th street. Daniel Hamm and Wallace Baker, out on bail with an assault charge against them, tell their stories. Another lad named Robert Rice speaks about Wallace Baker:[10]

The cops ran after those little kids
That didn't have anything to do with it.
One roller caught on the little boy.
He got him between his legs and was going to beat the little boy
On his head
When Wallace stopped the roller,
Then two of them jumped him.
At that time he was fighting with the rollers.
And from there a whole lot jumped him

> And everything was gone,
> It was a big scatter.

A lad named Robert Barnes says:

> We all tried to help Wallace Baker,
> And as we were helping him, more police officers
> came
> And they started pulling out their guns and aiming
> them at people.
> And one in particular, one colored roller, pulled out
> his gun
> And told Robert Rice that he was gonna shoot him
> dead right there
> On the spot if he didn't drop a garbage can.
> He had the garbage can defending himself, because
> the roller
> Pulled out his gun.

So here it is, testimony of open resistance, openly arrived at. The walls of the Friendship Baptist Community Center do not come tumbling down. Within them, rather, an aura of heroism begins to surround the young resistants. The social worker conducting the interviews says effusively that although there were only a few fellows actually involved, they represented every young man in America. Minds were made up that night to do something about it. The people were proud of the way they saw the boys defending themselves from the police that Friday afternoon. They were going to the courts and charge the City of New York with police brutaity.

CHAPTER TWO

Less than ten days later, Danny Hamm's mother learned that her boy, the wounds still aching and bleeding on his legs, was in the Meat Grinder again. He had left his house about a quarter after seven in the evening on his way to meet the lawyer who was representing him in the fruit stand case. He had just finished his homework for school. His mother told him it was time to see Mr. Senna, so he got ready and left."

MRS. HAMM

My oldest son he heard Danny calling me in the
    hallway,
Because I had just got up out of the bathtub and
    couldn't hear.
So he said Momma, I think I just heard Danny
    hollering.
So I said I don't hear anything.
So I guess about a minute later he say I just heard
    Danny holler again.
I said I don't hear anything, so we opened the door,
And we don't hear anything.
So I went and got into bed, 'cause I was ill at the
    time.
All at once a heavy knock on the door.
    Bangbangbang.
So I opened the door. I says yes?
And he says . . . a detective . . . I couldn't see his
    face too good,
Because the light was right over my door and at the
    time it was out,
So he says . . . Are you Danny's mother?
I said yes.
So he says I am taking him down for questioning.
So I said what for?

He didn't say anything. He just walk downstairs.
So I told my other son that . . .
No . . . I asked the detective what precinct you
    taking him,
He still didn't say anything.
I got dressed real quick and I went round to the
One-Thirty-fifth Street Precinct.
I thought that's where they were taking him.
And I was there and an officer told me they didn't
    have him.
My son Teddy went to the precinct on One-Twenty-
    third Street,
And he said an officer told him they didn't have
    Danny
And if he didn't leave they would arrest *him*.
So I went round to one-oh-seven West Hundred and
    Thirtieth Street
To try to get in touch with Mr. Senna,
And they say Mr. Senna just left.
So I call his house and his wife say he wasn't there.
I was just walking around.
I didn't know what to do.
I was a nervous wreck.
I didn't know what to do, so I came home because
    I started sneezing.
My son Teddy . . . he still hadn't come home yet.
I guess about twenty minutes after I got in the house
    my son came in.
I said they said they didn't have Danny there in the
    precinct.
He said I was down in the precinct on One-Twenty-
    third Street,
And they told me if I didn't leave they would
    arrest me.
I was sneezing real bad then and coughing.
So he went back to the precinct on One Thirty-fifth
    Street
And they still told him they didn't have Danny.
That way I didn't know what precinct Danny was in.

I was just a nervous wreck.

So me and Teddy decided to go to court to find out
if he was there.

For the fruit riot they didn't call me,

So I said for this they'll probably do the same thing.

Let's go to court.

We went to court and then we found out.

I couldn't tell that he had been beaten then,

But I know he was a nervous wreck because he was
just trembling,

And when I found out what had happened was when
I talked to him.

At two-seventy-five Atlantic Avenue in Brooklyn . . .
in the jail.

Because they wouldn't let me talk to him in
the court;

The judge refused permission for us to talk to
the boys.

Too many men in the back, the judge says.

Danny told me the detectives met him in the
hallway —

I think it was three — come up and they asked are
you Danny Hamm?

And he says yes and right away

Gun right to the head and slapping him up,

One gun here and one gun here . . .

Just all the way down the hall . . .

Beating him and knocking him around with the
gun to his head.

There is a special, an excruciating torture which
comes out of love. It comes mainly out of uncertainty
and fear . . . out of wanting to protect, in this case, and
not being able to find the object of the compulsion to
protect. One can have a rage to shelter, to enclose, and
when this is denied . . . Mrs. Hamm had found it unbelievable a few days before that the police would beat
a boy, her boy, all night long, and leave his hands looking
as if they'd stuck pins in them. And leaving his legs

covered with clots so he couldn't raise his trousers. Now she knew. It was no longer unbelievable what could happen in the Meat Grinder, but now it was she that was feeling the torture.

And the mother of Robert Rice. He had spoken up at the meeting at the Friendship Baptist Community Center. He had, in fact, implicated himself on the tape, saying openly that during the riot he had picked up a garbage can to defend himself, had demonstrated his will to resist. His mother too knew all about what happened at the Meat Grinder.[12]

MRS. RICE

My mother was home when they took him.

He was in bed, in fact, my mother was in bed also.

And she say when they knocked on the door she
   got up,

And they wanted to know if this was where Robert
   Rice lived.

She said yes.

So they wanted to talk to him.

So she called him and he said I'm in bed, let them
   come in.

They came in and asked him if he was at the
   Center . . .

'Cause they used to go to the Center and play
   basketball,

You know, in the evening.

And he said yes . . . you were there also.

And they said we want to take you down to the
   precinct for questioning.

So my mother said he's not going alone. I'll go
   with him.

They said no, we don't need you to go.

She said he's not going unless I go.

So she started to put on her clothes and she asked
   the detective

To leave, and he wouldn't leave.

He said he wasn't going out.

MRS. RICE

So she said you're going out of my house, you know.

And they wanted to search his clothes and
everything.

She says you don't have a search warrant so you're
not going to

Search his clothes.

So she asked him to leave again and he went outside.

And she put her clothes on.

She said it was three carloads of detectives outside,

And they wanted him to go in one car and she
in another

And she said no, I'll ride in the same car with him.

Robert said when they went into the precinct

They put him in front of this big mirror . . .

Which we know is a two-way glass.

They told him he could go home, they didn't
need him.

I went back to the precinct to try and find out why
they had

Arrested him.

The policeman that had arrested him would not
come and talk to me.

He told one of the other detectives to tell me
what happened.

So he came over and he said if someone assaulted
you

Wouldn't you want us to try to find what happened?

So he said we don't need him any more, you can take
him home.

I carried him home and the next day they came and
got him again.

They came about eleven o'clock the first night.

The next it was about eight, or a quarter to eight.

Then Robert was beaten.

He said they didn't hit him on the face . . .

It was like through the body,

On the legs, so it wouldn't show.

But I was at the precinct.

They had him for five hours and they told me he
 wasn't there.

I knew he was there.

It was one o'clock when they finally came down and
 said he was there.

They wouldn't even let us upstairs, my husband
 and I,

To the detective department.

Five hours I was waiting at the precinct, five hours.

One of the neighbors told me he was picked up.

Then they told me that night they were going to
 arraign him.

They didn't say for what.

I didn't break down, but I was very nervous and
 upset,

Being there and not knowing the reason why,

Because they don't give you any information.

I had called a lawyer during the time he was there.

And the lawyer called the precinct, because he told
 me on the phone

He couldn't come right there then

But he would call and see if they had him there.

And when he called they said no, they didn't have
 him there,

They had him the night before.

But at the same time he was there.

The lawyer came about a quarter after twelve

And they continued to tell him that he wasn't there.

And he had to speak of getting a judge, because
 you know

I had the license plate of the car that took him to
 the precinct.

But then the D.A. and Detective Sergeant Connor, I
 think it was,

Came down and they talked with him.

They admitted they had him, after the five hours of
 saying he

Wasn't there. So I went home.

I heard it on the seven o'clock news that they
would be arraigned
For homicide.

That word was a stone dropped on the mothers from
a great height. And this too was hard to believe . . .
harder and more horrible, something coming out of the
beatings and the torture, perhaps torn out of a bruised
mind, a bruised consciousness. They didn't know where
it came from, but they knew what it came to in the end—
the ultimate torture, bound in the straps, and then the
jolt of the electrodes* and then the flesh burned from the
inside out. Their voices tremble and break when they ap-
proach this part of the story.

The softest of the mothers is Mrs. Craig, as soft, as
deeply soft and plangent as all the mothers in the
world.[13]

MRS. CRAIG

My son Willie Craig was arrested the night of
the murder,
On the night of April the twenty-ninth.
It was raining.
One of my friends' daughters was at my house.
Willie was there, so I asked him would he walk
her home
'Cause she didn't have cab fare and I didn't have
cab fare to give her.
This was about . . . about ten-thirty.
So he left.
He and this girl left and went to One Hundred and
Forty-third Street.
About eleven o'clock I kept hearing a noise coming
from the roof.
And all of a sudden I heard somebody coming up
the stairs.
So I looked out the door . . . I had my door open . . .
I looked out of the door and there was some men
coming up.

*At the time this incident occured the death penalty for felony
murder was still operative.

MRS. CRAIG

I didn't know who they were at the time.
So one walked to the door and he asked me if this
     was where
Billy Craig lived.
I said Billy Craig?
No, there's no Billy Craig here. There's a Willie
     Craig live here.
Well, that's who we're looking for.
At that time a couple of them went up the end of
     the hall . . .
And down they came from the roof,
It look like about twenty of them,
And they come right in to ask me where was
     Willie's room.
I say it's back there.
So I took them back to his room.
They asked me where was he?
Well, I said, I send him on an errand for me.
Where was that?
I said One Hundred and Forty-third Street.
Where was that between?
I say between Lenox and Seventh Avenue.
Four sit there in the house and waited.
The others left, and I'd say about forty-five minutes
     later
One come up the stairs and say we got him.
I was on my way into the front room, and when I
     heard that
I turned around and come back.
And the others were getting up to go out.
I said you got him? You got Willie?
One turn around and said yes, we got him.
And my friend was sitting there and I said would
     you go down with them
And I'll be right on because I got to get my boots
     on and my coat.
So I went and got my boots and coat on and I went
     out the door.
Soon as I got outside a cab was there,

And I got right in the cab and went to the Twenty-
eighth precinct.
This was about eleven-thirty.
I walked in and I tried to talk to somebody,
Some of the detectives,
And everybody I would ask something . . . just a
minute . . . just a minute.
This continued until about five-thirty in the
morning.
Five-thirty . . . one of the detectives come out and
he called three boys off by name.
And he said the other mothers can go,
But these mothers stay for a little while.
So we sat there and they brought Willie out.
They sat him down at the desk.
So I asked, I said what are you holding him for?
He said for assault.
I said who did he assault?
That time Willie ask, he say who did I assault?
And nobody still didn't say anything.
So me and Mrs. Thomas, we stood there.
We stood around until about six o'clock,
And this detective he kept saying go home and get
you some rest
So you can be in court in the morning, 'cause we are
keeping these boys.
I didn't know why they were holding them no more
than just as assault.
I couldn't think of anywhere I could go for help.
I felt everything was hopeless.
A friend of mine downstairs, he heard . . . and my
daughter,
She was downstairs, in an apartment downstairs;
She saw the three boys on television.
So she ran up and told me about it and by the time
she could get
Upstairs to turn the TV on up there . . . it was
gone already.
She told me they were arrested for murder.

33

Let the pictures characterize these women further. These and their words. The tape runs on like an infernal machine. It will trap you if you talk to it a long time and you begin to tell lies. It reaches back and sinks deep and it spins on out of your consciousness. It abhors false notes. Shows them up clearly and rejects them, makes them sound raucous in the listening ear. There are no false notes here, only pure agony."

MRS. THOMAS

About eleven o'clock, or ten minutes to eleven,
Somebody knocked on my door,
And my youngest daughter went to the door and
    asked who is it?
And they said they wanted to know if Turkey
    was there.
So my son, he was there and he thought it was one
    of his friends.
He went to the door to see who it was . . . and my
    little daughter,
She was still standing at the door, she hadn't
    opened it.
And when he opened the door the detective just
    pushed the door open
And pushed my little girl up against the wall
And dragged my son and started to try to handcuff
    him.
Well I thought it was some of his friends wrestling
    or playing.
I didn't pay too much attention to it frst,
But when I looked back I saw there was still
    wrestling going on
Back there, and I said what's going on back
    there?
And I got up and went back there
And I found there were about ten or eleven
    detectives in the house.
One of them had thrown him down on the chair
And trying to put his hands back to handcuff him.

MRS. THOMAS   1473034

I had cleaned out his closet that day . . .
I had a couple of old coats on the floor by the
    garbage.
And they kept wrestling with him, so I ask the
    detective . . .
What you want with him? What are you trying to
    do to him?
So the detective say we just want to talk to him.
Talk to him about what?
Why are you wrastling him? Why are you trying
    to fight him?
So the detective say oh take it easy, take it easy,
Don't get excited.
And this same detective that was in the papers,
He went into the kitchen and picked up one of
    the jackets,
And he ask my son, he say where you get this
    coat from?
So my son say my mother bought it.
So he asked me where did I get the coat.
I told him where I got the coat from.
He said what is it doing here?
I said it was no good, it was ripped, it was torn from
    the pocket down,
It had been fixed, repaired, and it was too small.
I said I was throwing it away.
They finally put the handcuffs on my son
And they started going through the house, looking
    through the house.
They told me they would take him down.
So I said I'm going too, just a minute.
They told me I couldn't ride with them, that I had
    to come down alone,
And by me not having anything on, they had al-
    ready handcuffed him,
They didn't wait.
They didn't give him a jacket.
He didn't have anything but a sweater on.
They didn't give him a jacket or a hat or anything,

And it was raining and it wasn't too warm that
night at all.
And they took him out just like that with his
sweater on.
And one of the jackets the detective had picked up
off the floor,
He kept that in his hand, and they went out.
By the time I had my coat and shoes on
They were in the car downstairs.
They wouldn't let me get in the car,
I had to go to Seventh Avenue and get a taxicab
To ride to the precinct.
And while they were in the car my son told me
they says
Now act smart, we got you, now act smart.
And he said he was frightened
Because he thought they were going to beat him.
And when I got to the precinct they put him in
a room
And we sat out in front for a while, for about
an hour.
Then one of the detectives took me and my sister
and Mrs. Felder —
They had her boy, Ronald Felder —
And her husband and put us in a side room
And told us to sit there.
We sat there, oh, about two or three hours.
And I just get impatient sitting there
Because I didn't know what was going on with him.
So I go outside and one of the detectives come
And he ask me something about a raincoat.
He asked me did my son own a raincoat, so I
told him no.
So he went back in the room.
Then, I must have been there till about five-thirty
in the morning,
The detective come up and tell us they were
keeping him.
I asked them what for and they told me assault,

But they wouldn't tell me assault
On who, what, where, or anything else.
I stayed until six o'clock.
Then one of the colored detectives came out and he
    talked to me.
He said Mrs. Thomas, you should go home and get
    some rest,
So you can be fresh in court tomorrow.
You stay here you can't do anything. You'll be all
    fagged out.
He said I promise you your son will not be beaten.
He said if he be beaten I will have you charge
    me personally
With police brutality.
He said now you can go ahead home.
And it was about six o'clock when I left the
    precinct,
And my son wasn't beaten.

Now out of the antediluvian murk, the minds of
men clotted with primitive secrecy and suspicion, the
minds of policemen, things begin to emerge. Coats, old
coats. They are looking for old coats. There has been a
murder that day in a second-hand clothing store. The
account of it in the New York *Times* (May 1) is so
cheaply lurid that it would be laughed out of counte-
nance in a yellow journal. "A group of boys entered the
store just before 5:00 p.m. They took up positions
around the shop and began taunting the proprietors.
When one of the youths asked to see a suit Mrs. Sugar
replied they had none in his size. Another youth then
drew a knife and stabbed the woman once in the heart."

Who would believe this? What besotted mind
would believe that a woman was stabbed to death because she didn't have the right size in a second hand
suit?

Something else emerged the day of the taping. It is
curious, and somehow very sad, that nowhere in the
stories told previously by the mothers, or the boys, does

the face of the enemy appear. How frightening to have an enemy so powerful he is faceless . . . like Yahveh! So inhuman that when he takes off his coat and his badge he becomes invisible or the mere embodiment of inflicting pain. Now along with the coats came the face of a detective gathering evidence; gathering coats.

Everyone knows that the assembling of evidence to be presented in a court of law requires the most meticulous scrutiny and selection. A man's life could hang on his proven connection with some object held by the police in secrecy, handled with the utmost delicacy, and presented with the assumption that it has been acquired and kept with that higher law of justice which should make self-evident that the court and its officers are not killers out of ambition or caprice, but men of the greatest integrity.

The collector of the evidence against these boys, according to the mothers, was one Lieutenant Satriano, exposed, non-racially, on the front page of the New York *Times* of Monday, November 30,[15] as having been arrested on charges of possessing and passing counterfeit money. He was accused of having sold fifty $20 dollar bills, counterfeit, for about $150. "After interrogation at police headquarters by the Police Commissioner's confidential investigating unit, the officer is said to have admitted to the charges." (He has since pleaded guilty: *Time*, Jan. 13, 1965.)[16] "Part of the transaction in which Detective Lieutenant Vincent Satriano allegedly sold counterfeit bills to a confederate took place in the Brooklyn Police Headquarters, the Government charged yesterday . . . the Government's complaint alleged that Lieutenant Satriano turned over 50 of the bogus bills . . . in the detective squad room."

MRS. BAKER

I would never forget his face,
Nasty as he was that night in my house.
He didn't ring the bell.

He took his stick and just, you know, knocked on
    the door.
So I said come in.
Look like there was about thirty of them, you
    couldn't tell.
They were from the front to the back.
I have four rooms straight through.
When they first entered . . .
I have a rack in the hall where you hang your
    coats on . . .
They just took the coats down, looking at the coats,
Throwing them on the floor.
So I asked them what did they want? What was
    they looking for?
They didn't say nothing then, just kept looking at
    the coats.
They say I'm going to search your house.
So I said have you got a search warrant?
This old nasty one I saw in the papers,
He say no, I don't have a search warrant and I'm
    going to search anyway.
Well, he did.
I didn't know how many was there, I couldn't see
    myself,
Looked like twenty or thirty of them.
They were from the front of my place to the back.
    I have four rooms.
So they was all at the back under the bed.
So I asked them what they was looking for.
They didn't say nothing.
They just kept looking . . . flashing their lights.
I said well I have babies back there, three babies,
My three grand-babies they was in the back sleeping.
They didn't pay the babies no mind on the bed,
They just picked up the mattress, and the babies
    rolling
On top of each other,
So I was a little angry at the time.
I still asked them well, who is you looking for?

'Bout twenty minutes later they said Wallace Baker.
I said what you want with him?
They said we want him for assault.
I said who did he assault?
They never tell me.
They want to know where he is. I say I don't know,
    I didn't.
So I ask my oldest boy where is his brother?
He say I don't know. He asked Jimmy where was
    his brother?
Jimmy says I don't know.
This was the cop I saw in the paper.
Oh, they start pushing Earl around, my oldest son,
Shoving him around.
I told them take his hands off him,
I said he hasn't done nothing, what are you pushing
    him around for?
They told him . . . well, get your coat, you're
    going down.
So Earl got his coat.
I told Jimmy, you go to bed 'cause you got to go to
    school tomorrow.
Cop said to Jimmy, you get your coat, I'm going
    to take you in too.
So I said you ain't taking him nowhere till I get my
    clothes on.
Will you please step out of this room till I get
    dressed.
The one I saw, I don't know his name, in the paper,
Oh I'll never forget him. He wouldn't leave.
I had to get up. I had to put my coat on over my
    robe
'Cause he wouldn't leave the room till I, you know,
    got dressed.
So they took him down, it was about eleven-thirty.
We stayed there from eleven-thirty, I looked at the
    clock,
Till five in the morning.
They wouldn't let my boys go.

And this old cop that was in the paper,
He's the one that was just pushing my baby around,
Pushing him from one side of the wall to the other.
The guy that was in charge there, I don't know what
his name was,
The colored fellow, told him stop pushing him
around and leave him alone.
So I sat there till about five in the morning,
Then I brought Jimmy home.
And they still didn't let my oldest son go.
They held him until around twelve o'clock the
next day.
Jimmy's sixteen, that's my youngest son, and Earl,
he's twenty-two.
The babies, they was on the bed . . . the cops just
picked up the mattress,
They didn't even care about the babies,
And them rolling over on each other.
One was six months old, and Sharon only two.
They didn't even care about the babies.
This one I saw in the papers . . . he was the nastiest
one.
The colored cop told Jimmy, your mother told you
to go to bed,
'Cause you have to go to school.
He said you go back there and go to bed.
But this one in the paper said he ain't going to go
to bed,
I'm going to take him on down too. You get dressed!
So they took him down.
So Wallace said, at the time he was coming in the
house . . .
He had taken his girl to the movies
And he saw the policemen coming into the house . . .
I asked him why he didn't come in.
He said because of the way they had done beat him
on the night of April seventeenth.
He didn't know what they wanted to do to him.
He knowed he hadn't did nothing,

42

But you know you get beat up for nothing,
So he was just afraid.
I don't blame him,
I wouldn't have come in either.
And the next day they came back there.
I had walked out at evening.
Oh, they was in my house all night that night,
Because they was looking for Wallace,
Being Wallace saw them come in there. He was
   afraid.
They were just in and out all night.
Two cars just on the other side of the street, by
   the church,
You know the church faces our door.
They was in and out of my house all night like it
   was a subway.
They pushed me around too, they just walked all
   over me.
They didn't pay me no mind.
I didn't know where to go.
I didn't know what to do, where to turn.

Daniel Hamm, eighteen; Robert Rice, seventeen;
Willie Craig, seventeen; Walter Thomas, eighteen; Wallace Baker, nineteen; and Ronald Felder, eighteen . . .
all arrested, and later indicted and arraigned for a
murder which the police say was committed by one
stroke of a knife in a human heart by one bloody hand.
Why so many? Is this a kind of ratio of values; that six
blacks must face the electric chair for the death of one
white? Whenever a crescendo of racist fear and guilt
begins to build in the white community, it seems that it
must always be resolved by a frenzied hue and cry, brutal
arrests, and hysterical trial of *multiple* black defendants
accused of a crime so monstrous that the whole apparatus
of the state backed by a totally terrorized and convinced
public opinion can be brought into a direct onslaught
against them. There were the Scottsboro Seven, the
Trenton Six.

MRS. FELDER

They were *all* guilty, it was said. It is an excellent tactic, to be sure. The more accused, the more potential betrayers, cavers-in, skirt-clearers; the more to get tired of grillings and outright torture; the more put under the sweating process, the more varied and specific, the more inventive the "evidence" will become. In two men accused of a common crime the temptation of each to blame the other for whatever accusation is being laid against them is enormous. With four or six, the temptation proliferates immeasurably. There is sure to be one that is soft, one that can lie pathologically, one whose loyalties cannot stick at the sight of impending death.

And a multiple accusation of this sort can fix an ugly stain on a whole race or nationality. If six Irishmen kill a Jew, if six Jews kill a Pole, if six Poles kill a Negro, if six Negroes kill a white . . . the guilt is flung in the face of a whole people. For one Irishman, Jew, Pole, Negro to commit a crime of violence is a daily occurence, no one ascribes any particular significance to the race or the nationality involved. When the guilt of a deed of common violence is affixed to many, acting in concert, it takes the obscene dimensions of ritual bloodletting."

MRS. CHANCY
(RONALD FELDER'S AUNT)

Ronald's arrest was from the home.
When they came for him I asked them what did
    he do?
They said nothing: we just want him for a
    investigation.
One of the policemen tried to be right nasty.
Ronald was in there reading a book.
I was laying on the bed; my husband was
    sleeping . . .
And the other little one was in there.
And when he came in . . .
It wasn't one, it was about fifty,
And all out front lined up with detectives and
    police cars.

And when they came in and they really find out
    that he was home
They ran in here like somebody was crazy.
I didn't even count them because I got so excited.
I didn't know which way to turn.
I said to them what happened, and Ronald got his
    jacket.
He walked over by that trunk
And that's when one of them took his billy and
    push him.
And I walk over and I got in between and I said
Now wait a minute, don't you push him around,
'Cause if he commit a crime he will be punished.
There wasn't no need of them beating him up
    before the time.
And one of the other cops tell him take it easy,
    take it easy.
'Cause you see, I would fight, you know.
So they say it wasn't necessary for me to go down,
So I got dressed and I went on.
Again I ask Ronald what did you do?
He said I didn't do anything.
Well, why are they picking you up, I said.
Well I don't know.
One of the policemen feel him in here.
Open up his clothes and feel him in here, on his
    heart.
And he say well, this kid is calm.
And my other little boy, which was twelve, he was
    sleeping
At the time,
And they wake him up and want to know does he
    know anything about it.
I told him no, the kid doesn't go around with these
    boys
Because he is too young.
And the detectives they insist that he must go.
They take him, a twelve-year-old boy,

Make him wake up, make him get dressed and take
    him down.
Another thing; they say they searched every parent's
    house
And they take something out like the Indians use.
They didn't even search this apartment.
They didn't take anything out here 'cept James,
    Ronald and me,
And they took me because I refused to let the
    children go alone.
And when we got downstairs they said the children
They must go in one car and me in another.
I axe them well, where are the children going?
They say in this car, and I say if they go here I
    go too.
So he said no.
I said don't tell me, if they die we all three die
    together tonight.
And when I got down to the precinct I kept saying
I wonder what it is, I wonder what it is.
They don't give me no reason whatsoever why they
    pick him up.
Then one of the detectives say to me what you
    think happened?
A man was stabbed serious and a woman was killed.
So then I said what time was that?
It was before five o'clock
I said what you mean, this kid was nowhere around
    there,
I know where he was, he was at home, I talked to
    him on the phone.
And about one o'clock, my little boy was in the
    precinct room
Sleeping.
They asked all parents to go into another room,
And when we go into this room, they wake up James
And take him in for questioning.
So while he was in the room this detective come out,
And he say to me

James is the only one that can free his brother.

So I said what you mean, free his brother?

Because James said his brother said he know who
do the killing.

And I said how could James tell you?

This child he don't even go around with them!

Then he asked me would Ronald talk with me . . .

Or would he get angry with me if I go in and talk
to him?

I say if he do, it would be the first time.

So I went in the room and I start talking with him
and I say

Tell me the truth now, 'cause this is a thing you
don't cover up

For your mother.

I say now the truth must be told.

He said Sadie, I'm telling you the truth,

I didn't do nothing and I don't know nothing.

So then, after I keep questioning him and asking
him,

This detective come back in the room and he said

Look at Ronald, look at Ronald, what kind of a
child he is.

He is clean all the way through.

But look at the company he keeps, just look at
his company!

CHAPTER THREE

The worst ordeal of the mothers was yet to come. The press, the radio and television had been building up a kind of horrified lynch mob in the rest of the city against Harlem. The phrase about the long hot summer coming on was taken as a direct threat against the whites. Every act of casual rowdyism involving black people was reported as an atrocity story. The Negroes were beginning to be described as completely out of control, tearing up subways, molesting and raping white women. White neighborhood vigilantes organized into roving patrols stopped and questioned every black man straying out of his home block. New York sounded to the rest of the country like some frontier town helpless before uncontrollable violence stalking its streets. The panic built up like an infection accelerating into visible putrefaction.

Then, when the second-hand store murder took place, the sore seemed to burst. The six black boys arrested for the crime finally personified all the doubts and fears of the white community. People in frenzies of fear called the mothers on their phones shouting black bastards, black bastards at them. Threats were made to bomb their homes and to kill a hundred niggers for the one white woman that was killed.

In Harlem itself a glacier-like detachment took place between the mothers and their neighbors. Mrs. Thomas says, "Everybody turned their back on us and gave us the runaround." Mrs. Hamm went to the NAACP and they told her they wouldn't touch the case with a ten-foot pole. The local Democratic Club wouldn't have anything to do with it. Somehow the press had been able to infect the whole community with a sense of shame so profound that the people began to actually believe what was being said about them . . . things that they had been able to disbelieve and bravely ignore since slavery times. Somehow the press had been able to implant in them a new form of original sin ... that they were killers because they were black. Walking the hostile streets of their home place, riding the subways to visit their boys in the Brooklyn prison, the mothers saw in every newspaper in the hands of reading strangers the hard bloody rain of invective and accusation falling on the heads of their sons, saw it proliferating a thousandfold as every new edition whipped up the silent, waiting, hating lynch mob of white New York.

And the police still kept their heavy hand on them. Lieutenant Satriano came to the home of Mrs. Rice after Robert was put away, with a search warrant.

MRS. RICE

He was supposed to be looking for a dagger.
In doing so he broke the dresser, the couch, the arm off the couch.
And the mattress on the bed —
In turning it over he ripped the whole side of the mattress,
And he was very nasty with my mother.
He wanted to go up in the closet and pull down boards
That had been hanging there for the last twenty years.
And he said it was his job, he had to do this.
And he went through all the clothes and threw them on the floor.
He wanted to know why Robert had so many clothes.
So my mother told him, my husband and I, we worked,
And we bought him clothes.
He just threw them down on the floor and stepped on them.

The same atmosphere of repression, pursuit and duplicity was applied to the younger children.[18]

MRS. CHANCY

We were sitting on the stoop one day
And little James was out there playing, and he say
Oh Mommy, I forget to tell you, you know those
people,
They take me down . . .
What people take you down?
He said the police they take me down to the
courthouse
Or someplace downtown and they made me sign
a paper.
And then he tell me this happened two days before
Without my knowing a word about it.
They went to the school and picked up my little boy
Up out of the schoolroom.
Took him downtown, kept him downtown from
about twelve to four.
First thing they bribe him with candy,
Next thing they bribe him with a ham-sandwich.
So James said he was scared because they had him
all in this big room
And they asked him what did he know about
the murder?
He told them he doesn't know anything.
So then they asked him well, where was Ronald at
the time?
He say Ronald was at the fish market around the
corner here.
So they told him well, we don't want to know that
story,
We want to know wasn't he before the store where
this murder took place?
He said he was scared because they were always
talking real fast
And it got him scared and he was afraid they would
beat him
And he told them yes.
That was my other little boy, but that child was
right here in

This house when that other thing happened.
The little boy thought they were going to whip him.

The lynch mob was led by the New York *Times* in full cry, with the publication of racist slanders against the people of Harlem reminiscent of Julius Streicher's attacks on the German Jews. When Wallace Baker gave himself up composedly to the police and was charged with homicide, the *Times* (May 5, 1964) promptly tainted him with a guilt so monstrous, so bizarre, that no ordinary motive for his conviction was necessary.[19]

The Police are investigating the possibility that he was a member of a gang of about sixty young Negroes, who, after being trained to maim and kill, roam the streets of Harlem, attacking white people.

Not only did they originate such stories, but they gratuitously republished invidious comment from other sources, equally hysterical, but important in driving wedges of animosity between minorities.[20]

Yesterday's edition of *El Diario La Prensa*, a Spanish language paper often critical of police dealing with Puerto Ricans and Negroes, carried an editorial in which it said, "It is horrifying to learn that the action [the murder] is suspected to have been a premeditated attack by a band of Negroes on whites solely for the reason of race." (New York *Times* May 5, 1964)

It seemed as if the *Times* was caught in the grip of a hysteria which demanded the speedy immolation of these six boys to save a city it felt was, like ancient Thebes, under a curse. A sub-headline on May 1, giving the first report of the arrest of the boys, read: A RACIAL MOTIVE IN RECENT ASSAULTS IS INVESTIGATED.[21] Nobody seemed aware that this was the real racism, turning a white city against a black community. People have said for years that if fascism comes to America it will be called anti-fascism. Possibly when racism comes to the *Times* it is under the banner of anti-racism.

No wonder the people of Harlem began to turn their backs on the mothers of these boys. They got it from all sides. The accusations of racial murders roared through the entire metropolitan press (with the curious exception, possibly, of the *Daily News*") like a forest fire out of hand. Listen to the strident hysteria of the New York *Times* of May 1:

> **The attack may have been the latest in a series of incidents in which militant and organized Negro toughs have assaulted whites with seemingly no motive . . . Police are investigating a number of recent killings and assaults in Harlem which seem to be the work of racists.**

There were said to be as many as four hundred in these gangs of teen-age killers, each pledged to train ten juniors for lethal action. The mothers of Harlem stood accused of carrying the seeds of murder in their very wombs. Whenever a child is born into that world, he now has to carry on his back, along with every other social liability known to man, the stigma of being a potential killer, an instinctive killer, of whites because they are whites; a killer because he is black.

The *Times* and the rest of the metropolitan press had become to the New York Police Department as the Voice of America is to the State Department. In every report of an arrest, of any incident of violence, in Harlem the lead paragraph began with some sickening but carefully phrased assertion that it was an act of racist hatred. The *Times* is the worst offender in this, because of the lethal quality of its poisoned cream-puff style. Its Harlem crime stories usually began "A detective disclosed . . . " How genteel this sounds, and how much better than the usual "alleged," because "disclosed" means that the detective *discovered* or *revealed* that which was a fact, an actuality."

> **A detective disclosed that the attack on the storekeeper might have been the latest in a series of incidents in which militant and organized bands of**

Negro toughs have assaulted whites with seemingly no motive. (New York *Times,* May 1, 1964)

The evidence or actuality thus "disclosed" is generally offered by "a detective who asked that he not be identified." Under these ground rules, all Negro children arrested for some alleged criminal act can be tainted beyond ordinary human doubt and compassion by any anonymous accuser in the Police Department issuing the statement that the accused were "identified as members of the Blood Brotherhood, an anti-white gang said to be operating in Harlem." Incidently, how can a gang be merely "said" to be operating when the accused are positively identified as being part of it? It is the intellectual as well as the moral rot of this onslaught that is so disgusting.

There never was such a crying of havoc over the crimes against Negroes, whether committed by black or white criminals. But the ever-increasing pathological narcissism of the whites demands that any crime committed involving them or their property must be the ritualistic act of a "hate gang," performed in envy of their superiority. And we only want to be *loved!* All who injure us do it only from hate—not because we are fat and scant of breath, or because we are dim-witted and inexcusably careless in the flaunting of our worldly goods, or because we are slow to move, overburdened as we are with the accumulated glut of a white-affluent society! We are hurt because we are misunderstood. Love us or we will kill you is our cry.

The major assault upon Harlem in the *Times* was written, naturally, by a Negro, Junious Griffin. The story of how his now notorious "killer gang" series came to be written is in itself a horrible example of how the good and the innocent can be brutally manipulated for the sake of some small expediency, the sensation of a day. With all the ponderous weight of the *Times* behind it—with its liberalism, its reputation for truth-telling, for meticulous research, for searching and fearless journalism—the condemnation of the boys so clearly stated in this series pressed the last vestiges of hope from the mothers' hearts.

The series began like the braying of the trumpets of doom, with a double-column, front-page article on May 6 headed: ANTI-WHITE HARLEM GANG REPORTED TO NUMBER 400. SOCIAL WORKER SAYS ITS MEMBERS ARE TRAINED IN CRIME AND FIGHTING BY DEFECTORS FROM THE BLACK MUSLIMS. *BY JUNIUS GRIFFIN.*[14] The story, said to be based on information given by an unnamed male researcher for Haryou, flatly connected the Blood Brotherhood, the boys arrested for the fruit stand incident . . . and the second-hand clothing store murder.

> The gang last clashed with the police on April 17 on the east side of Lenox Avenue between 128th and 125th Streets. Two members of the gang were arrested in that clash and were later implicated in the fatal stabbing of a white woman on April 29.

Then there is a quote from the so-called "Haryou tape." The man who made the tape so venomously manipulated by Griffin into an instrument for the extinction of all sympathy for these boys feels utterly betrayed by him. He is a professional interviewer, but more than that an artist, a musician of surpassing talent, who uses the sensitivity with which he reveals the form and pulse of a musical work of art to probe and, in the kindest sense, to play on the outraged sensibilities of the people of Harlem until the deep sad horror of their daily existence rises in a kind of monochromatic *lacrimosa* of bewilderment and hurt.

A white man, a civil rights worker who knew Griffin, had been disturbed by Griffin's first *Times* story about the Blood Brothers and wanted to convince him that they did not exist. He felt that the immediate cause of the obvious unrest in Harlem was two new laws, the No Knock and the Stop and Frisk laws. The people in Harlem felt that the laws were particularly addressed toward them, and in the hands of an agency as corrupt as . . . well, as corrupt as Lieutenant Satriano . . . they could be used badly against them. For example, the No Knock law permits the police to kick down the door of a home, enter it bodily, and then present the search warrant. Harlem people feel that this allows the police to plant any incriminating evidence they need in the resulting confusion. The Stop and Frisk law could have a similar effect in giving the police the power to stop anyone on the street and manhandle them, without papers, and with every opportunity to plant evidence in the pockets of whomever they chose to affront in this way.

The civil rights worker knew that the Haryou interviewer had a tape which he felt showed the indicted boys in a good rather than a bad light, and he asked the Haryou interviewer to play it for Griffin. The interviewer agreed, because of his firm conviction that the boys arrested were not guilty of the murder . . . and for a good reason:[25]

"To me, if kids know the police don't like them and are constantly watching them, they are not going to act in this way. While I was interviewing these kids the sergeant was walking by the window and looking in. Another police officer kept glancing in, and after we had finished the interview and we came outside there was three or four of them on the corner, looking at us. Now the point I wanted to bring out to Griffin was . . . You mean the kids could be that stupid? . . . and if anyone had heard the tape and got an idea of the thinking of these kids . . . these kids are not going to turn around on the twenty-ninth and commit a murder! Now this is the point I was trying to get Griffin to develop, but I found out that Junius Griffin was only doing the job the New York *Times* wanted him to do."

Over and over again Griffin questioned the interviewer about murder gangs. The interviewer repeatedly denied their existence. At one point he did admit that he had heard rumors about them, but carefully explained that this was merely part of the constant psychological warfare which goes on in Harlem against the unrestrained power of the white oppressor. Griffin kept saying he had talked to this or that teen ager; he had heard them call each other Blood Brother!

The interviewer's reply is touching: "I said well, man, blood brother is not really a derogatory term. And it's not a new term. I remember when I was a kid, and I'm thirty-five, blood brother was a term we used to use. We got it from the Indians. Meaning that we were from the same mold . . . we are suffering from the same conditions. This would make us blood brothers. And to sanction it we would prick our fingers and the blood would run together. This was based on the Indian thing . . . because when I was coming up all that we used to go to were the Westerns. And even today musicians address on another as hey, blood brother! . . . or soul brother."

Griffin then insisted that the interviewer bring his tape down to the *Times* office for transcription, so he could meet his "deadline." The interviewer protested that this operation would have to be cleared with Haryou. Griffin called Haryou and got permission by convincing the official that use of the tape would bring credit on the organization for being on top of questionable police activity in Harlem and implied that he was going to do a job highly sympathetic to the Harlem point of view. He met his "deadline." His article came out the next day, damning, possibly to death,* the six lads as members of a murder gang of Blood Brothers whose existence was now testified to by an accredited Haryou investigator.

Many of the quotes in the article were deliberate falsehoods. Some were evilly twisted in meaning . . . there was scarcely a point which the interviewer had put in defense and understanding of the slandered people of Harlem and the poor boys literally in the shadow of the executioner's chair that Griffin did not disfigure with error, either of principle or of fact. The whole article

*Again it must be made clear that the death sentence was still in effect.

was a loose discharge of venom which made the interviewer sick at heart. He asked the white man who had been present at the discussion to prepare an affidavit of Griffin's inaccuracies and malignancies, which was done and sworn to and which relieved him, somewhat, of the awful feeling that he had unwittingly set the feet of these boys on their last mile. When the *Times* was taxed with this deception, instead of displaying some decent contrition, they replied that they had confirmation of their slanders from "another independent source."

But even in these doctored articles, Griffin is forced to mention an astonishing amount of evidence negative to his lethal thesis. [26] The Youth Board denies the gangs, or said it had no proof of their existence. Haryou denies it. Most of Harlem's middle class deny it. Police Commissioner Michael J. Murphy, now resigned, "has repeatedly denied that any pattern of brutality exists . . . nor will he publicly acknowledge the existence of the gangs." That *publicly* is a weasel word, but that may have been inserted by Mr. Griffin himself, hell-bent to shore up the collapsing structure of his penny-dreadful. We should not be concerned, in a newspaper account, with what Mr. Griffin or Commissioner Murphy know *privately. If six boys' lives depend on it, let such damning evidence come out in the open and be tested by the rules of evidence and a dispassionate search for the truth.* Conrad Lynn, the famous defense lawyer, requested a meeting with Griffin after the first *Times* articles appeared in order to see evidence supposedly in Griffin's hands proving the existence of the Blood Brothers. According to Mr. Lynn, Griffin agreed to a meeting at 229 West Forty-third Street. "He hasn't appeared. I am still waiting. He is afraid to face me after what he has done."

And this is what he has done, among other things. He quotes a mysterious seventeen-year-old "Blood Brothers' Leader" who, with a bewildering lack of the racist loyalty which is supposed to be his ruling passion . . . provides an almost unbeatable prosecution motive for the conviction of six boys. [27] "Maybe these boys had something done to them by white policemen, or maybe some other white person had done something to him, and he can't get back at that person. Well, he'll take it out on anybody he sees." And then the youth himself was supposed to go on describing his own feelings against whites and to say that he was training a number of small boys in the use of judo and karate against policemen, "or in a fight with Whitey or with Puerto Ricans."

It may be true that this unknown, and so far unknowable, black boy was practicing a little psychological warfare, a little verbal terrorism on the gullible *Times* man from downtown, scaring the bejesus out of him. Why not! Boys are like that, and his gory talk is typical of American juvenilia since before Tom Sawyer and Huckleberry Finn. But for Griffins to use this loose talk, this childish running off at the mouth so that it would obviously help to convict this boy's own alleged "Blood Brothers" is a callous act of inhumanity before which ordinary morality stands aghast.

The boy may have been full of a genuine hate: every black man worth his salt feels his muscles flexing with anger as he looks about him at the unending denials and insults. But the Negro is of a noble race and he will *nobly* dare to be free! He may yet have to stand his ground at some Lexington Green, but he's not going to start by plunging a knife into the heart of some poor pathetic Hungarian refugee, as alien as he is in this land of a few winners and millions of losers, where the poor are always losers and the winners always weep: weep because they are not loved and people want always to hurt them, they think. It is conceivable that men have killed because a storekeeper does not have the right size in a suit . . . [28]

> When one of the youths asked to see a suit, Mrs. Sugar replied that they had none in his size. Another youth then drew a knife and stabbed the woman once in the heart. (*New York Times*, May 1, 1964)

. . . but up to now, this motive, so clearly ascribed to the boys by the *Times,* seems to have been unrecorded in history.

The other angle of Griffin's attack came from his assertion that the tape proves that the boys interviewed of it—Daniel Hamm, Wallace Baker and Robert Rice—were "with the Blood Brothers who took part in the April 17 fruit riot." This tape is in my hands at the moment; there is not one whisper of evidence that any "Blood Brothers" were involved. The boys do call each other brother, which Griffin and the *Times* have defamed into a crime, but people used to talk loud and long about the brotherhood of man, and still do, on Sundays and in the one week in the year we call Brotherhood Week.

The tape, far from revealing implacable hatred in the consciousness of these boys, evokes love. At the time it was made, the boys were regarded as local heroes, not toughs nightly running amuck in the streets of Harlem. They were supposed to have thrust their bodies between the police and the young, pre-teen-age children being beaten by clubs. Some, the parents of these children perhaps, would consider such interposition an act of love. It sounds that way in the deeply aggrieved voice of Robert Rice: [29]

> More rollers came in and they was taking their
>   guns out
> And pointing them at little boys.
> And one little boy have a bump up side of his
>   head from a club,
> From where the policeman hit him on his head.
> He has the scar there on his head now.
> And *nothing* is being done about that.

To hear Robert Rice's voice breaking in pain as he describes the blow struck at the child's head puts the listener about as far from simple hate as he can go.

And as for their hatred of whites . . . there is Fecundo Acion, a Puerto Rican seaman. The Negroes do not, as far as I know, consider Puerto Ricans as members of their race. But Wallace Baker's voice as he describes the beating of Acion shows anguish and horrors as great as when he suffered and intervened over the beating of the Negro children. [30]

> There was an old man that was in the crowd.
> Now when the old man saw them beating Frank,
> He tapped the cop on the back and was asking him . . .
> What were they doin',
> And they turned around and whipped that old man down to the ground.
> And now it's been two days and we haven't seen
> Or heard from the old man; he's still in jail.
> Nobody don't know nothing about the old man.
> Nothing. And they don't have nothing on him.

Again on the tape, clearly for Griffin to hear, were these remarks of Robert Rice. [31]

> There was this colored policeman that took his gun out
> And say he was going to kill me.
> So I got out of the way.
> And I was running . . . the rest of the brothers . . .
> They was taking the white . . . the brother white . . .
> They put him in the police car with Daniel Hamm.

And of course the "brother white" was Fecundo Acion, the Puerto Rican seaman. None of these boys seem to have the dangerous illusion that the good guys and the bad guys can be divided up into blacks and whites, as Griffin says they have. The deepest feeling that emerges from this tape is not hatred for the police but concern over the "old man," the "brother white." It rises again and again, in a beautiful cadence of sympathy and concern. [32]

> And about the old man, the old man
> He wasn't fighting . . .

He didn't do nothing but ask a question,

And he got his head busted open for nothing.

This is said by a boy named Robert Barnes, and as he finishes there is a low, introspective murmur in the background. The interviewer says, "Huh? What was that?" And the deep, soft, solemn voice of Wallace Baker says, in the long, tenderly halting cadence of grieving:[33]

He get that just for a question.

He get his head beat up just for a question.

No reason at all, just for a question.

Over and over again the interviewer asks the boys if they were treated any differently in the course of their jailhouse beatings by the Negro policemen. They always said no. He persists . . . "What I am trying to say now, do you feel that the Negro policemen felt the same way about you as the white cops felt?" The boys said definitely they did. Daniel Hamm said: [34]

And the reason I could say that is because

Robert Rice told one that he was the same color as we were

And it didn't make no sense for him to blow our brains out.

And he told Robert Rice he was not the same color as we were.

In other words, he didn't have the same color skin as we had

He was light-skinned. [35]

ROBERT RICE

Yeah, naturally I went to talk to the colored roller . . .

So I asked him well, brother, what's going to happen?

He said well, first of all, we are not alike.

You don't look like me and I don't want no part of you.

> Where does that leave me? What I going to
>   do now?
> I can't say nothin'.
> He's against me now!

But it would be false to endow these boys with a permanent aura of sweetness and light. They are militant, filled with the wisdom of street boys who had to wade through corruption on their way to kindergarten; they are politically sophisticated and they know the reasons behind their own plight and the blocked directions of their own destinies. [36]

DANIEL HAMM

> They don't want us here.
> They don't want us . . . period!
> All they want us to do is work on these
> Penny ante jobs for them . . .
> And that's it . . .
> And beat our heads in whenever they feel
>   like it.
> They don't want us on the street
> 'Cause the World's Fair is coming,
> And they figure that all black people are hoodlums
>   anyway
> Or bums, with no characters of our own.
> So they put us off the streets
> So their friends from Europe, Paris or Vietnam ---
> Wherever they come from —
> Can come and see this supposed to be
> Great city.

But the "great city" was under a curse. New York was New Thebes and the *Times* was its Oedipus. The city was under a plague and the visitors from abroad who rode through the streets of Harlem would be affronted and made cynical by its poverty while on their way to the great celebration, the crowning monument, the bench mark and the showcase of our business civilization, the World's Fair of 1964. They would have to see; there was no escaping it, the rotting houses, the un-collected filth, the scenes of turbulence rising from a frustrated humanity unable to escape from constriction and squalor. And when the visitors would ask for an explanation of this sickness in the very shadows of the strong towers of steel, glass and light lifting their arrogant apostrophes of power, they would have to be told that this was a long, long sickness, a hundred-year sickness, sometimes thought to be incurable.

It was a plague that brought to people, because they were black, a life in which 50 percent of them lived in houses which could be officially condemned as unfit for human habitation, in which mothers and fathers stayed up all night to keep the rats from eating their babies . . . which operated on the minds of their children with such stultification and hopelessness that they found no healthy, no aspiring incentive for the use of their minds . . . in which six times as many people are murdered than anywhere else, in this great city, and twice as many babies die at birth. And for a palliative, the greatest traffic, the most successful business in narcotics, pain-killers, agony-easers, happiness pills, unrest-snuffers-out, life-destroyers in the world is carried on.

The *Times* has all the Aristotelian qualifications for the tragic hero. For the most part it is "highly renowned and prosperous . . . but not pre-eminently virtuous and just" . . . without vice or depravity but constant in some error of judgment and frailty. And like Oedipus, it suffers for the city, for its people and for itself. And in May, at the start of the long hot summer in the city under a curse and plague-ridden, the *Times* seemed to act as if finding the murderers of white people in Harlem would lift the plague in time for the city's purification before the admonishing eyes of a visiting world. [37]

OEDIPUS

**What is the rite
of purification? How should it be done?**

CREON

By banishing a man, or expiation
of blood by blood, since it is murder guilt
which holds our city in this destroying storm.

From May 1 to May 11 the *Times* never let up in its shrill denunciations and incantations, its triad of fear and rage built on the "Blood Brothers," the murders of whites, and the arrest of the six boys. The same phrase, the same paragraph used over and over again like the hammering of an alarm bell in the night.

The police already suspect that members of the gang are responsible for four Harlem murders, all of white persons. (May 6)

The police already suspect that members of the gang are responsible for four Harlem murders, all of them committed against whites. (May 10)

And other incantations:

Confirmation of the gang's existence was given last Saturday by a high-ranking police official in Harlem. The police said the gang members became eligible to use the letter X when they seriously kill or maim a white person. (Junius Griffin, May 1)

More than 40 Negro police undercover men moved into Harlem yesterday to investigate an anti-white gang, six of whose members are suspected of the murders of four white persons. Six youths described by the police as being members of the gang have been arrested in connection with the murder of Mrs. Magit Sugar last Wednesday. Three of them, Daniel Hamm, Wallace Baker and Robert Rice, are charged with the slaying. Six were also questioned about other murders in which all the victims were white. (May 7)

Then, on May 11, the New York Branch of the NAACP challenged the attorney general of the state and the city law enforcement agencies to prove that these gangs existed. The rest is silence. The daily incantations stopped. The exorcising ceremony had not worked.

Nobody at all came forward to provide evidence so clear and indisputable that these boys could be given a speedy public trial by an impartial jury and be confronted with the witnesses against them. They are in prison yet, with no trial on the docket, nine months after their arrest.*

And like Oedipus, the *Times* blinded itself, burned its empty eyesockets toward common justice and mercy. It is neither just nor merciful to incessantly repeat the prosecution's unproved accusation before a trial in a country where the arrested are considered innocent unless found guilty by their peers. It is utter blindness to common justice and mercy to unremittingly repeat in its columns the unanswerable arguments of the police persecution in the state and district where the crime has been committed and from which the jury will be drawn, the witnesses summoned . . . and where all these, including the defense lawyers themselves, fall under the spell, the power and threat of these incantations of unquestionable guilt.

Part of the blindness lies in the irony that in the same stories which admittedly fail to prove the existence of the murder gangs, reasons are given to call them into some future existence. Harlem, says Griffin, without stressing the point too strongly, has "wall-to-wall cops." These, unlike the Blood Brothers, quite visibly exist. They are organized into a Tactical Patrol Force of some twenty thousand men which seems to have no other purpose than to suppress, harry and arrest Negroes. Griffin says they "saturate" the area of the 32nd precinct where the troubles dealt with here are centered. "They are said to be arresting," he says in his article of May 29, "scores of persons whom the regular patrolmen would have to overlook." [38]

How do these policemen look to the people of Harlem? Griffin describes them as all over six feet tall, with specialized training in judo and karate (those skills making it possible to kill a man without the use of

*Their trial finally began on March 19, 1965 and concluded July 7, 1965. They were found guilty of murder.

weapons when a black man learns them, but when provided to the police called simply "instruction in human relations"). Griffin says the Tactical Police Force puts into effect what Commissioner Murphy calls his "philosophy of police work . . . the substitution of a show of force for the actual use of force."

It never takes very long for the show of force to become the use of force, but why are the people of Harlem required to put up with even a "show of force"? Technically, black Harlem is not an occupied country. We have not fought a war there so bloody that we have to leave white mercenaries to "saturate" the area or as a "peace-keeping" force. And as for defining them as mercenaries, let us consider again the example given by Lieutenant Satriano, the peddler of counterfeit bills from the privileged sanctuary of the detective squad room of the Brooklyn Police Headquarters, the man who shoved Mrs. Baker around, who tore up Mrs. Rice's mattress, who banged on Mrs. Hamm's door with his stick, who gathered the "evidence," with or without a search warrant, for the state. The Lieutenant has a home at Hartsdale, New York, valued at $35,000. It has a barbecue in the back yard, a 1963 Cadillac and a small car in its garages. When Lieutenant Satriano was arrested, his fellow police say he had $1,300 of the legitimate variety in his pocket. Of such are the ranks of the mercenary.

Or is he not working for hire and killing his man (as he did in 1956) and being decorated for it, but unselfishly upholding in and for Harlem the Constitution, the Rights of Man and the Great Society into which the people of Harlem will be admitted when they overcome someday? The fact is that Lieutenant Satriano and the men he commanded, the Negro police officers of rank and the men they command, act every day in Harlem as if its people had no rights in the Constitution, not even the right to due process of law, which the police have to respect.

Now, why is it that the people of New York living outside its ghettos cannot understand the crushing weight of these conditions on the people of Harlem? Is it because the black people, having found a new militancy, are no longer acting like perpetual victims but more like what they actually are—oppressed in an occupied country? The white residents of New York are perhaps the most politically aware people in the nation, and the black people at their sides know the same things, feel the same wants, suffer the same doubts and fears, and learn the same lessons they do.

So why do they not understand that to saturate a people with wall-to-wall invaders with arms in their hands is an egregious insult? That it is, to Harlem, living in a police state? Why can't they understand that the power, the wealth, the political supremacy and subtlety of the New York Police Department has brought forth, inside its apparatus, a whole system of propaganda and self-justification? Why can't they understand that this new and vicious imputation of a murderous racism to the inhabitants of Harlem serves to frighten off liberal support and rational solutions, and leaves the final solution of that bruised society's discontents up to the night-stick, the gun, and, as too many black people have come to feel, perhaps the gas chambers.

CHAPTER FOUR

The boys I have never seen. They are entombed over there in Brooklyn, living in a nightmare so prolonged and intense that when they speak one cannot know what region of their private hells they are speaking from. Would they see in my white face the mask of the oppressor they carry deep in their remembering blood, and sit across from me with silent, implacable hate? Who knows what wounds would open and bleed again as they looked at me? Perhaps a truthful relationship with me and my white world — their world of torturers, cheaters and scorners, peddlers of the ideology of lies we call humanism and democracy has been beaten out of them for good. Their consciousness of me as another member of the race, the *human* race, may have been shattered like glass. It has been fragile at best. They have the consciousness of *one* race when they are little, but we soon beat it out of them. Perhaps it still exists in the gene: this is our only hope.

Their mothers see them in the jail, talking back at them from a cage. They always ask the same question: When are we going home?

They are being beaten in the jail. They tell their mothers that it is a common practice for the guards to stop the elevators between the floors of the prison and then give them a working over with billy clubs and gun butts. Lawyers have protested to the Supreme Court that these boys have been beaten to extract confessions, motions have been made to force open testimony by the victims, open rebuttals by the police, all fair and square, where the people in whose name the boys are being confined can themselves judge which side is telling the truth and which side they should be on. This is always denied . . . the hearing. The charges never get to that point of prominence where the police have to publicly deny or even discuss them.

The first concern of the boys was who would be the lawyer to conduct their defense. A man in a fix like this, on trial for his life, wants someone he can trust and be easy with. Mrs. Craig hurried over to Atlantic Avenue in Brooklyn to see her son Willie after being denied a single word with him in the open court. [39]

MRS. CRAIG

I had to have the proper identification
In order to prove that I was his mother
Before I could even see him.
He was in a cage, and I had to look through a small
    glass like this
And I had to talk to him through a phone, over
    a phone.
He said he didn't know anything about this —
What they had charged him with.
He asked me to get a lawyer.
I told him I was trying all I could to get him one.
'Course he knew that . . . you know . . . that I don't
    have money,
Didn't have money . . .
So that I was just completely blank.
I didn't know what to do.

But Willie Craig had a lawyer. In the case of all six boys, one lawyer after the arraignment had signed a notice of appearance for all of these boys. This meant that when any other lawyer, chosen by the mothers, came to the clerk of the court and asked permission to see one of the boys in jail because one of the mothers wanted him to, the clerk would say well, unfortunately Mr. So-and-So has a notice of appearance in here. We can't let you compete with him, so you can't see him. [40]

The lawyer who did this had reason to believe that he would be appointed by the court to defend these boys as counsel for indigent defendants and be paid $2500 per boy. This one lawyer, as a political appointee—for it is the custom in the New York courts for the assigning judge to appoint counsel approved by the Democratic Party Clubs—has the power to prevent all other lawyers from seeing the prisoner, even though the prisoner wants to see those lawyers. This is one of the most vicious aspects of the system of court-appointed defense counsel. This naturally prevents other lawyers who suspect police coercion may have taken place from interviewing the prisoners and being able to see if they are carrying any welts or bruises. They could demand that a physician check evidence of beatings, but this they cannot do because one man has filed a notice covering all defendants.

The people of Harlem have a deep distrust of court-appointed counsel. They know they are almost invariably hangers-on at Democratic Clubs, many of them without offices, who depend on this sort of handout for a living. These assigned counsels do not spend much time with their clients. They have a history of doing a bare minimum for them, sometimes not even seeing them from the first arraignment to the day and hour of the trial itself. They usually assume the client is guilty, and their form of defense is to get their clients to make a plea of guilty on a lesser charge.

The boys in prison had a deep distrust of their assigned counsel. After the beatings and attempts to extort confessions from them, after weeks spent by all of them in solitary confinement and never seeing a lawyer to whom they could make a complaint, they became so hostile to their lawyers, they would not, finally, even talk to them. Talking with the other prisoners, they came to believe that anything coming from or sanctioned by the state was suspect. They felt, as most people in Harlem do, that it was inconceivable that any judge, owing his office to political circumstances, would appoint a lawyer that the prosecutor would object to. In New York City, the district attorney is one of the top political satraps; he is proud of his record of over 90 percent convictions. What judge, they felt, is going to appoint a lawyer to put him down, to raise a storm against him in a case so unremittingly advertised far and wide as solved?

There is a pleasant fiction, to be sure, that the judge, out of compassion for a poor client, will appoint some leading light of the bar to defend him. Nobody really believes this, and in the case of the boys one lawyer was appointed who fell dead in the courtroom because he was a chronic alcoholic, never seen sober in the courtroom during all his years of practice, and yet appointed by a benign justice to defend the life of an eighteen-year-old boy.

The mothers themselves shared the common prejudice against court-appointed lawyers or even Legal Aid Society lawyers. [41]

MRS. HAMM

I didn't think this was a good thing.
The reason I didn't like was 'cause . . .
I had a friend . . . she was in the same position,
And they gave her a Legal Aid lawyer
And the lawyer just sat there.
Didn't get up and say one thing —
Didn't get us to say one thing in the boy's defense.
So therefore . . . I was in the court when this
    thing happened,
And so by them appointing me a Legal Aid
I felt my son would be in the same position.
That's the reason I didn't want no Legal Aid.

Mrs. Rice and her husband, a little more prosperous than the others, inquired around for a lawyer. [42]

We have a district leader, Mrs. Watson.
She didn't come to see me,
But she sent word to me that I should use a Legal
    Aid lawyer
Because it didn't make sense to try to spend
    money . . .
To save Robert, to try to get a lawyer to help him.
So I sent word back to her if it took the rest of
    my life

And I have to work night and day to have what I
    want to have,
I would do this . . .
Anyway, it seems like the judge didn't want us to
    have our own lawyers.
Even if we could afford it,
Because Judge Calkins, when we went down with
    our lawyer,
He called me to the bench first
And then he called my husband to come up,
And he said the costs of the court and the appeal
Would run you into so much money . . .
You would save to spend three hundred dollars a
    day for the minutes,
And I think it would be very foolish to spend your
    life's savings
When the state will appoint you two lawyers.
We said no, we would rather have our own lawyers,
But it seemed that they didn't want this
Because they did the same thing to Mrs. Craig . . .
They didn't want us to have the lawyers that we
    wanted
From the beginning.

This attitude of the futility of defense, on top of
the great offensive directed against the Harlem community, began to corrode the mothers' hopes for their
children's liberation. They repeated over and over again
their assurance of the innocence of the boys. [43]

MRS. CHANCY

The police say at the precinct it happened at
    five o'clock.
But at four-thirty I was at my job
And I said gee, I haven't called the children yet,
And I went into the room where I was working and
    put on my shoes.
It was twenty-five minutes to five, and I called up,
And Ronald was right here, and I ask him
What he want me to bring home to cook.

He said nothing, you know I'm satisfied with
    anything you fix.
So I said I'll tell you what, you want me to bring
    home some beef
And fix you some okra soup?
He said that would be fine. This was twenty-five
    minutes to five.
I call the children every day about this time
When they get home from school.
I know he was home. I dressed and took the train
    from Twenty-third Street,
And I stopped right here at the Garden Market.
I got the beef and I came straight home, I didn't
    stop anywhere.
It was between five-thirty and twenty minutes of
    six when I got here,
And that's why I know what happened . . .
But in the morning at court . . . they kept him!
That's the thing that got on my nerves more
    than any.
When they asked the detective what charges they
    had against the children,
The detective said the only charges they had
    against them
Was that the witness say they see them leaving
    the scene.
So the judge said we couldn't hold them on that.
And then the district attorney said hold them on
    felony assault,
And so they could hold them!
We never seen no witness, never told who the
    witness was or nothing.
This colored detective say well, how you think we
    got Ronald's name?
A woman came to us. We didn't go to them. She
    came to us.
And who this woman was nobody know because
I never seen this woman in court.
That was the same night of the arrest.

A woman told the detective Ronald's name and
   that's how
They picked Ronald up. But they never produced
   the woman!
Never.

The mothers have their own incantations or litanies
rather, because they are filled with innocence and hope
instead of fear, guilt and hate. "

MRS. THOMAS

Mine was home . . . all that afternoon.
He was home that day because it was raining,
And I wanted to go do my shopping for groceries
And two of them was there.
And I made him stay and mind those two
While I was at the store.

MRS. CRAIG

And my son was with her son.
My son Willie Craig was there and they were fixing
   wheatcakes.
Willie didn't leave till about quarter to four,
And then he went on to Mrs. Thomas's right around
   the corner.
It was raining.

MRS. BAKER

Wallace told me he was at his girl friend's.
She lives in the Bronx.
She said he was there.

MRS. HAMM

Danny was home doing his homework.

MRS. RICE

Robert was home then, and then he went to the
   Center.

The mothers clung to this accountability of the
presence of their sons at the murder time. It sustained
them during the jailhouse visits, when their boys would

come to look at them from the cage with hardly a word of greeting or communication, but with their eyes fixed silently in a trance of remembered pain, agonizingly beyond their reach, beyond their mothers' power to succor or relieve. It sustained them during the long periods when the boys were put in solitary and they could not even see their faces, and knew, moreover, that this punishment usually followed some act of resistance to the guards coming from abuse or beating. They were hopelessly resigned to the appointed counsel until they heard that . . . [45]

MRS. HAMM

The lawyer tried to confuse the boys!
Each boy he would talk to . . .
Like he would talk to my son Hamm.
He said Hamm, you might as well confess
Because Mrs. Thomas' son has, and he said you
    did it.
And he said Thomas, you might as well confess
Because Baker said you did it.
And Baker, you might as well confess
Because Rice said that you did it.
This was our defense attorney . . .
The Legal Aid lawyer doing this!

MRS. BAKER

We didn't know where to go,
We didn't know where to turn
Only when we came around here to Bill,
And that was a week or so later, maybe two weeks,
When Mrs. Thomas said I got to find somebody to
    help these boys!
And I think, Mildred, you the one that found Bill,
And we came round here and talked to Bill.

The Bill referred to here is William Epton, a Negro—or a black man, as he may prefer to be called. He was the head of the Harlem Defense Council, at 336 Lenox Avenue, New York. He is a radical, a communist spelled with a small *c*, and also functions at the same address as the Harlem leader of the Progressive Labor Movement. If coming to this page has suddenly alienated the reader I have overcome with my gentle persuasion so far, it will have to be. *I* didn't go to him; the mothers went to him on their own initiative because there was nowhere else to go. They say this over and over again. This is not an apology for Mr. Epton's role here; he doesn't need any. But it is now a fact of American life, along with the beating of children in shifts in precinct houses, that those who totally reject this form of society and call for its transformation are getting to be the only ones able to carry on a dialogue of aid and comfort with its oppressed.

Mr. Epton suggested that they talk their situation over with Conrad Lynn, the civil rights attorney, with offices at 401 Broadway, New York. [46] Mr. Lynn I did go to, many times, because it is my considered belief that Lynn is the only man left in these times with the oratorical power, the openness, compassion, and above all the innate sense of righteousness and prophecy that was the hallmark of the great abolitionists of the 1850s—Frederick Douglass, Garrison, Phillips, Charles Lenox Remond and Theodore Parker. In thirty years of constant communication with these last, not astrally but by an almost daily wrestling with and meditating over their words and their works, I have not encountered their like until I went one bitterly cold winter night to a small hall in Boston — there were barely thirty people present—to hear about a dramatic confrontation of the Ku Klux Klan by armed black men led by Robert Williams in Monroe, North Carolina.

Mr. Lynn was the speaker and he laid a spell upon us all, a spell that only those with true oratorical power can evoke, in which the listener is swept out into a rushing stream of words, sensations, even passions, in which his own landscape vanishes and all is new around him, and he feels carried against his will and almost fearfully to some newness and change himself. He is swept over the dam of his own limitations and prejudices and can never get back or feel the same again. Perhaps I heard this because I have been listening for it so long; but I have heard him many times since, and he has never failed to take me up and fling me into new and instantaneous decisions of daring to be freer and open with other people . . . absolutely open with everyone, friend or enemy, as Lynn himself is.

It is easy for me to understand how the mothers must have felt sitting before him for the first time, exhausted of hope, crushed in spirit, utterly functionless now as protectors of their children. Lynn is a small man, and black, and this smallness and blackness gives the effusions of indestructibility and fearlessness that he radiates a higher quotient of truth than if he were big and white and Zeus-like and out of touch. He has a way of topping his crescendos of attack with laughter, not bitter or acrid in the least, but almost joyous, exulting that his enemy, in the demonstration of his most hurtful power, has made himself so little and mean that history will dismiss him as a pompous absurdity, a flyspeck on the rails now thrumming to the onrush of human advance.

I can well imagine that the mothers smiled there in his office for the first time since the blows had fallen on them. He is too good a lawyer to tell them he could save their boys regardless, but he did say that this case of the so-called Blood Brother murder is one pre-eminently showing the influence of dominant prejudice against a minority which is deprived of defenses; also that actual hard proof of the crime by the boys is missing, and the prosecution is depending on the existing state of prejudice to obtain conviction. As for the police reconstruction of the crime, Lynn feels it was wholly drawn from one of the *Times's* sophoclean dramatizations, or incantations, which would not even ring true if clearly labeled as creative fiction. But if no lawyer is willing or permitted to go into the background and reveal the social pressures behind the prosecution, the boys cannot get an adequate defense. "

"I felt that this should be an occasion," Conrad Lynn says, "with these young boys facing the electric chair, where they should have the right of counsel in whom they have confidence. But I knew the judge would refuse to appoint any lawyer except the particular political hack in the Democratic Club whom they wished to favor at the moment. However, I told these mothers I would talk to other committed civil rights lawyers and see whether they would attempt with me to get appointed by the judge to defend these boys. So I contacted William Kunstler, who is one of the attorneys for Martin Luther King, Mary Kaufman, a celebrated lawyer who defended political dissenters, Sam Nueburger, a very noted New York criminal lawyer, and Gene Ann Condon, who had worked in the office of the corporation counsel and knew the operation of the political machinery. We then applied to the court for permission to be appointed attorneys for these boys and be paid the regular stipend provided in the law for indigent defendants.

"And in the first instance, Mrs. Craig, mother of Willie Craig, wrote a letter to the judge and asked that Gene Ann Condon and myself be assigned to defend her son. The judge wrote a letter to her in which he said that he was taking care of the appointment of counsel and he would accept only the procedure that had been applied in the past. The lawyers that he would appoint would be satisfactory. And he didn't even bother to tell the mother the names of the lawyers that were to defend her son for first-degree murder.

"Thereafter Gene Condon appeared in court with Mrs. Craig and made an oral plea to be assigned by the judge. She was refused. William Kunstler made the same motion; he was refused. Then Mary Kaufman and Sam Nueberger pleaded and were refused. We heard through the mothers that the boys were being maltreated, beaten in the jail. I demanded through a motion in the court that I be permitted to see Willie Craig as attorney for his mother. I wanted access to him at all times, even though the court would not appoint me lawyer. After a

Mr. Conrad Lynn

great deal of effort and publicity, the court allowed me to see Willie Craig. There he told me that there was constant grilling of the boys and all of them had been beaten at one time or another. It was the custom of the guards to stop the elevators between the floors of the prison and then work them over. This was a common procedure.

"I made a motion in the Supreme Court in Brooklyn for a writ of habeas corpus, in which I was joined by the other lawyers, to free the boys upon the ground that they were being denied the right to counsel. The right of counsel, as we conceive it, means the right to counsel of one's own choice. It is not the right to counsel that the court appoints, counsel that as far as the accused knows may be collaborating with the district attorney, counsel who is in the good graces of the prosecuting authorities and the court. This is not the counsel that the accused whose life is at stake would want to choose. Therefore, I moved for a writ of habeas corpus for Willie Craig, unless he were permitted to have counsel of his choice. The second ground was that he was being beaten by the police and the jailers in an attempt to compel him to make a false confession. This was a denial of the right of the accused to have a fair trial and be permitted to confront the witnesses against him.

"My main argument was that the practice of the courts in assigning lawyers against the wishes of indigent clients was to practice a difference in defense based on property qualifications. A poor man who cannot afford to hire a lawyer for his defense against a first-degree murder charge, where the average cost would be at least five thousand dollars, would be denied the counsel of his choice, but a wealthy man who can afford to pay the thousands of dollars has a much better chance of surviving. Therefore there is, in effect, a denial of the equal protection of the law, based on a class distinction."

Although Lynn and the others knew that to storm headlong the entrenched power of political privilege would be a long intricate struggle, a precedent set in the Scottsboro case and upheld, in tendency, by many subsequent Supreme Court decisions offered the mothers their last best hope for the lives of their sons. The Scottsboro defendants had court-appointed lawyers, but they were able to interest in their defense Sam Liebowitz, a top criminal lawyer who had the courage to face the strong Southern prejudice against black men accused of raping a white woman. The Supreme Court ruled that Liebowitz could defend them and that they were not to be burdened legally with the errors they claimed were made by their court-appointed counsel. This was the first great decision in which the Supreme Court said the right of counsel means the right to counsel of one's choice.

Courtrooms in New York have a certain frigidly antiseptic quality, very different from the run-down, dusty, dark walnut and threadbare plush traditionalism of Massachusetts courtrooms. They are rather like waiting rooms in outpatient departments of charity hospitals . . . spotlessly clean, efficient and palely decorative . . . deceptively composed antechambers of pain. The judges look like doctors on the hunt for disease. They are restless and alert, their minds are an active file of old cases, old symptoms. They sniff the air for lesions in the body politic. They seem to crouch rather than sit monumentally in judgment as in the old mold. Perhaps this wary look of the hunter comes from the long service many of them have put in as hunters of men for the state as prosecutors, punishers. Judge Julius Helfand, sitting on the habeas corpus hearing on July 1, had been a district attorney for twenty-seven years . . . had been a hunter, against the hunted. When the lawyers made the pleas for the boys, and the mothers, who were in the courtroom along with myself, he would wave aside citation after citation, saying I know that, get on, hurry up: acting as though he were engaged in a contest, as if he were on the other end of a ping-pong table, obligated to return every shot, field every challenge, without a moment's hesitation or deliberation. He forced the defending lawyers to play his game, talk faster, cut corners and suppress pertinent facts and arguments they had intended to introduce.

In court with him, and on his side of the barrier, was the usual battery of upholders of the state power, including the state's attorney general or his major deputy, I am not sure which. The crucial nature of the question here, this plea of poor people in deep trouble and without adequate means to carry out a life and death struggle, was apparent only in the earnest and very eloquent, even passionate arguments of Lynn, Mrs. Kaufman, and a brilliant young attorney, Elinor Fisher, representing the Kunstler office. They were saying that when people are poor and helpless, because of it they need some measure of compensating attention and deliberation. The note struck by those resisting the plea was rather shockingly callous and outdated. In a phrase heavily redolent of the tragic 1930's when a whole country became pauperized, the attorney general said if you let these people pick their own lawyer, pretty soon the indigents in the hospitals will be picking their own doctors and surgeons.

Judge Helfand obviously agreed, because after the arguments had ended, like a man taking an examination or playing a quiz game in which he knew all the answers in advance, he turned confidently to a law book in which he said there was a citation which covered the case perfectly and contained all the thoughts and conclusions he required on the subject. It was the case of the *People . . . V. Fuller,* Court of General Session, May, 1901. Its simple brutality deserves quoting.

PAUPER-CRIMINAL, ASSIGNMENTS OF ATTORNEY . . .

A destitute defendant, charged with murder in the first degree, can have no part in selecting the counsel authorized to be assigned to him by the Court and paid for by the County. It seldom happens that a defendant is arraigned, charged with murder in the first degree, without many applications for such assignments being made to the Judge before whom the arraignment is held by counsel claiming previous retainer, or especial familiarity with the case, or claiming to represent the wishes of the accused, or his family, or some other equally cogent reason. It has, indeed, been a matter of common rumor that zealous "counsel" have sometimes offered to divide their prospective fees with the family and friends of the accused in consideration of their inducing the accused to ask the Court for their assignment as counsel. The accused, in prison and with a relatively limited acquaintance as to the capability and suitability of counsel and oppressed by the gravity of his situation, is often but poorly able to choose or recommend. It is the plain duty of the Court to protect the defendant from such improper influences, and to permit him, under these circumstances, to suggest counsel to be assigned by the Court, and paid for by the State, is to open the door to such grave abuses that I am unwilling to encourage it. There is doubt whether a defendant able to retain and pay his own counsel will ever do so, if he knows on his application the Court will assign and the State pay them. It follows, therefore, that if the Court is to assign counsel, it should do so free from any prompting or suggestion whatsoever, either by the defendant or by counsel desiring such assignment. The defendant is wholly free to select his own counsel, but if the Court is to assign, and the State to pay, then the independent selection by the Court, by removing the temptation, will prevent the improper solicitation of such assignments by means both despicable and unprofessional, and will, at the same time, permit the assignment in proper cases of counsel who are eminent, able and honorable. [48]

I have neglected to note down the name of the man who said this, but since Judge Helfand finds it exactly to his taste, and lets the opinions of a man given in 1901 answer the anguished pleas of young boys born over forty-five years after it was given, let it stand as Judge Helfand's opinion. When it was given, the Negro was the victim of medieval torture. In 1900 and 1901 some twenty-seven Negroes "suspected" of various crimes were reported in the press [49] as having been lynched, mutilated, and/or burned at the stake, so that it is possible that it was an act of grace at this time to let a black man get into the courtroom at all. But we have made some progress since then; the world does move.

But the minds of men who become prosecutors and judges never seem to change; the attitude of the judge as expressed here is pure colonial paternalism. For them the black man or the poor man can never grow into adulthood and responsibility for his own destiny. He is always a dupe and a victim, and it is always the duty of officials like Helfand to protect him against himself. What would these boys on trial for their lives now care about the competency of counsel . . . no, all they want to do is get someone to represent them who will split the fee with their relatives!

This attitude runs deep in the consciousness of certain people in this country. It is a rational trait among the whites. Jefferson Davis, [50] sitting on the first of the Un-American committees, to inquire into John Brown's raid on Harpers Ferry, queried a supporter of Brown's, Joshua R. Giddings of Ohio. Mr. Giddings had stated before the committee that there is a higher law than that of Mr. Jefferson Davis and the courts which says that wherever any human exists "there is the right to live; the right to attain knowledge, the right to sustain life, obey the laws of his Creator and enjoy heaven or happiness."

Jefferson Davis was quick to sniff out the revolutionary heresy in this and to characterize and bracket, in the same way the bureaucrats do today, the poor and the black . . . with the criminal and insane. "Did you," he asked, "in inculcating the doctrine of a law higher than that of the social compact, make your application exclusively to Negro slaves, or did you also include minors, convicts and lunatics, who might be restrained of their liberty?"

Giddings, in reply to this, pointed out that insane people and criminals have to be restrained for the safety of the people, but the Negroes were the people themselves, and it is the object of a people's government to secure them in the enjoyment of life and liberty.

Davis rejoined: "And if the law of the land should deem it equally necessary for the safety of the country to restrain other persons, does the higher law resist?" And he developed his point more specifically by asking if minors and apprentices should not be restrained . . . and here is the heart of the matter! The black and the poor in this country are now and always have been treated as irresponsible children and apprentices, except that there is a time limit on these; they can and will grow up and be consistently treated as citizens and men or women. Even the poor man becomes rich occasionally and is given some responsibility for his own destiny under the law. But the Negro never can reach adulthood in this country, never become wholly formed, except by token here and there. True, he can become rich, but he can never become unblack.

This tragic exceptionalism is the rot at the heart of our society. It never ends. It is the same in Washington, D.C., in 1860, in New York courtrooms in 1901 and 1964. The black man or the poor man is forever "poorly able to choose or recommend" how he shall live his life, or how he shall defend himself from sudden death. It is forever some rich white man's duty to be free to act *for* him, to protect him from "improper influences." This is the eternal justification for chattel slavery in the old South, peonage in the new, for whipped heads in Harlem and apartheid in the white republic of South Africa.

This is why Judge Helfand dismissed the plea of six boys about to go on trial for their lives to have counsel of their own choice.

CHAPTER FIVE

After this cruel denial, the mothers returned to their own homeplace and began a different and vastly more fruitful form of struggle, defending and explaining their sons in the only place in New York where this tragic struggle stands honest and revealed, the streets of Harlem. Under the guidance and support of the Harlem Defense Council they talked to their neighbors in street meetings every Saturday. Their reception was warm, attitudes had changed. The New York police force, after sending in secret hordes of plainclothesmen disguised as dope addicts, winos, street cleaners, salesmen, window cleaners and taxi drivers, and sitting interminably at every corner in unmarked cars, were unable to turn up any evidence whatsoever of a Blood Brotherhood murder gang. The New York *Times* and Junius Griffin, in response to the eminently reasonable challenge from the New York Branch of the NAACP [51] to prove the existence of the Blood Brotherhood stood silent and rebuked as liars and malicious mischiefmakers against a whole community.

The police seem equally unlucky in producing witnesses against the boys. Their chosen defense lawyer claims that the only witness now available is an eight-year-old girl who was supposed to be at the second-hand clothing store at the time of the killing. Four young girls from the ages of fourteen to sixteen were subpoenaed to appear before a grand jury to testify about the case, but were actually taken to the office of the District Attorney without their parents' knowledge and grilled about the boys. They knew nothing.

The shock of the pain, helplessness and futility of their position began to wear off the mother's bruised consciousness. For five straight weeks people signed up at their street meetings to help their boys. They collected money for the inevitable appeal, for they were sadly certain that the counsel assigned to their sons would enable the D.A. to get another easy conviction. Some days they collected as much as forty or fifty dollars. This showed great sympathy and interest, for the people of Harlem have to express their largesse in terms of nickles and dimes. And then another policeman, this time off duty, knocked another black boy to the ground. This time not with a club but with bullets from his police pistol, pumping a shot into his body as he lay dying.

This was in Thursday Morning, July 16, 1964. The killer was Lieutenant Detective Thomas Gilligan. The boy was James Powell, fifteen, a summer student at the Robert F. Wagner School. The boy had been in an argument with a building superintendent who has been squirting him with a hose, "to wash the black off." Some say the policeman shot Powell twice on the ground, and then turned him over with his foot. When the police came in numbers to the scene of the killing, the students coming out of the school demonstrated angrily against them, throwing bottles and cans.

The next day at noon, the Congress for Racial Equality organized a demonstration at the 67th Precinct house. Some four hundred students marched there from the school that Powell attended; to 67th Street, between Park and Lexington. There they ran up against police barricades and patrolmen by swarms. The following evening a street rally to protest the killing was held at 125th Street and Seventh Avenue. After the meeting many of the people began to congregate at the 28th Precinct on West 123rd Street, to demand the arrest of Gilligan for murder. The police, after setting up barricades, began to charge the crowd with nightsticks and guns, beating and dragging off the demonstrators.

It was the fruit stand riot again, on wide screen. A barrage of bottles began to come down on the police from the roofs. The Tactical Police Force arrived on the scene and Harlem was sealed off from outside traffic.

Police began beating and shooting in a saturnalia of violence which left the streets slippery with blood; the blood flowed so unrestrainedly, the blood of black people, unarmed and in their home streets, that at Harlem Hospital sawdust was strewn on the floor because there was no time to mop it up. The riot the police set off in Harlem has now passed into history; it need not be recounted here. It was complex and needs more research and perspective to judge it as a historical event. But it is clear it began with a police killing.

The police version of the killing is that the Powell boy was coming at the officer with a knife. Eyewitnesses say no; some say Powell was rushing out of the building unarmed; there is some talk that he was carrying a garbage can cover. In this discussion it is not the details of the incident but its typicality which is important. It is far more horrifying and truer, I believe, to realize that Gilligan *was* doing his duty, that he was confronting a circumstance in which he had been taught that killing was not murder. Someone up there in the police pentagon must be teaching, literally brainwashing policemen to shoot to kill whenever a black person assumes a threatening posture toward them whether the person is armed or not. What Gilligan did, off duty, was pure reflex to instruction and orders; to draw his gun and fire into the body of a fifteen year old boy because he was threatening and because he was black.

The greatest proof that Gilligan was "following orders" comes in his clearing by a grand jury after testimony for six weeks. The official report is sixteen hundred pages long; the only section revealed to the public by the district attorney is a fourteen page extract. If the full report could be forced under the public eye, there is no doubt in my mind that pre-reasons, pre-justification for Gilligan or any other police officer, on or off duty shooting to kill, form the bulk of the "testimony." If not, the police authorities can clear themselves by offering this report in full to scrutiny.

There is a dominant psychology in this country, a kind of new Calvinism brought in by our self-guilt, and well illustrated in our foreign policy and cold war and nuclear arms postures, that everyone that is not "like us" is full of some innate depravity, full of the original sin of wanting to destroy us, usually with their bare hands. This forces "us" to confront them with half-drawn weapons at every moment, like some cheap Western gun-fighter who assumes that every man with some strangeness on him is waiting to shoot him down the minute he can get the drop on him.

There are times when this even transcends racial lines. It is most clearly illustrated when Robert Rice, being threatened once by a Negro policeman with a gun in his hand, went later to another black man and said they were both the same color and it didn't make sense for one to blow the other's brains out. Robert was shocked when the "brother" said, "First of all we are not alike. You don't look like me and I don't want no part of you." Robert Rice thought this rebuff came from the policeman's being of a lighter color than he was; but it is not that. The policeman was different because he was a policeman. His training, indoctrination, and subsequent brutal, even murderous reflexes set him off from every other member of the community, black or white, who does not have this license to kill as a duty.

It seems to me that the real difference is that many policemen are a little sick, or very sick, and that there should be an immediate psychiatric examination of any police officer who clubs a man after he is handcuffed, after he is arrested, or of any policeman involved in a fatality which would be out-and-out homicide if done by a person not carrying a badge. Sadists not only cannot restrain themselves from hurting people, they cannot tell the simple truth about anyone. They even hurt people in their talk; merely sitting in the witness box they are often able to ruin a man's life, or cause his death without lifting a finger.

Because of this killing, the mothers were no longer

able to defend their boys on the streets of Harlem. The Harlem Defense Council called for the following Saturday to be devoted to a demonstration against police brutality which would have for its high point a mock trial of Lieutenant Gilligan for murder. There was universal agreement that there would never be a real trial. The city authorities issued an injunction forbidding this or any like demonstrations from taking place. The irony is that the streets of Harlem represent perhaps the last area of the country where the people gather voluntarily and talk about what is happening to them, instead of seeing themselves and what they are supposed to want through the predigested, distorted establishment-oriented and approved eye of the television screen. But this last enclave of a people's democracy was crushed.

The Harlem Defense Council was troubled about their duty under these circumstances: should they abdicate the only rights left to them in a bourgeois democracy, the right to complain about it somewhat? Conrad Lynn was called in to give his legal opinion of the silencing injunction. He said he felt that when people could not walk and talk in their own neighborhoods at a time of crisis and agony, a last-ditch struggle had to be carried out. He advised them to hold the meeting, defy the injunction as unconstitutional, and offered to put his own body, his life, his fortune and his sacred honor as an officer of the court into the demonstration.

"The meaning," Conrad Lynn says,[52] "of the savage suppression of the people of Harlem now becomes clear. Thousands of police with a staggering variety of pistols, submachine guns and bazookas occupied the black community, ostensibly to prevent any repetition of the riot, actually to cow the Afro-Americans into total submission. Consequently it was most essential that a small band of black militants march on July 25, 1964. They had undertaken the task of showing their black brothers in the rest of the country, and the oppressed people everywhere, that the black man could no longer be frightened into submission, not in Harlem or the Congo.

"On Lenox Avenue that Saturday afternoon, the black masses witnessed the alternative to fear and sub-servience. The major 'Negro organizations' in convention assembled on 125th Street and tried to do Marse Charlie's bidding in getting the march called off. When words failed, James Lawson, so-called black nationalist, offered black goons to the police to smash up the march. But the thousands of Lenox Avenue residents who swarmed out of their rat-infested tenements to cheer on the little band frustrated these plans. A new perspective for the numberless little people was being revealed."

Conrad Lynn and Epton linked arms with another leader, William McAdoo, and walked down the street, against the injunction and into arrest and possible assault. They were arrested; the injunction was upheld, and the mothers were again cut off from their compulsion and ability to defend their defenseless children. A few days later, Epton was arrested and jailed on a charge of "criminal anarchy," and is now released, pending trial, on $10,000 bond. The mothers' two great champions were now under harassment almost equalling their own. [53]

By now, their case, or specifically the cases of their imprisoned sons, had begun to assume that grandeur of dimension which sometimes provides an elevation from which a view of a whole society and its continuity may come into focus with a frightening clarity. In my own exploration of these events, with their highly drama-tic moments of pity and fear, I have come to the conclu-sion that there is a prevailing attitude in this country summed up many years ago, and correctly, by the honest racist Judge Roger B. Taney of Maryland, Chief Justice of the Supreme Court of the United States. In announc-ing the majority decision of the Court in the famous Dred Scott case, Taney said, on the argument that Negroes were people, as mentioned in the Constitution: [54] "In the opinion of the Court, the legislation and history of the times, and the language used in the Declaration of Independence, show that neither the class of persons who had been imported as slaves, nor their descendants, *whether they had become free or not,* were then acknowledged as a part of the people, nor intended to be included in the general words used in the memorable instrument. They had, for more than a century before, been regarded as beings of an inferior race, and altogether unfit to associate with the white race, either in social or political relations and so far inferior that *they had no rights which the white man was bound to respect."*

Does anyone looking honestly at Harlem or any Northern ghetto, or at Mississippi or any Deep South area, really believe that the blood shed by the Negro soldiers, the abolitionists, and those reluctant defenders of the American equalitarian dream, in the war against slavery has invalidated this decision? Look at the denial of due process to the black man, the beating, the punishment without trial which almost invariably takes place in that bloody interval between his arrest and trial. Look at the trial itself; with the denial of proper counsel, of counsel of his choice, because he is poor! Look at Judge Helfand's regurgitation from the benighted past that poor defendants, and they are almost always black men in New York City, have to be protected from "improper influences." And above all, look at the injunction laid down by the city itself, the most liberal, supposedly, in the world. Think of these words, these restrictions being applied to any white community . . .

. . . Restraining and enjoining the defendants, their officers, directors, agents, members, representatives *and all other persons whomsoever,* known or unknown, active in their behalf, or in concord with them . . . in any manner, or by any means from assembling, gathering together, convening, parading, marching, demonstrating or acting in concert in the public areas in the borough of Manhattan, City of New York, bounded by 110th street on the south, 155th Street on the north, Franklin Delano Roosevelt Drive on the east and the Hudson River on the west, and attempting to . . . induce or persuade . . . civil rebellion and the overthrow of lawful government . . .

Is not this the sort of thing we object to in South Africa? It happened in New York, it described Harlem. The protest against it by white New Yorkers was beneath notice. Obviously the people in Harlem have no Bill of Rights that anyone has to respect. And not only the people of Harlem, but "whomsoever, known or unknown."

Judge Taney was highly prophetical as well as being a good sociologist who understood his countrymen of his color. He went on to say that no state, North or South, could elevate the Negro to a position of full citizenship, because: [55] "If they were so received and entitled to the privileges and immunities of citizens, it would exempt them from the operation of the special laws and from the police regulations which they consider to be necessary for their own safety. It would give to persons of the negro race, who were recognized as citizens in any one state, the right to enter every other state whenever they pleased, without pass or passport, to go where they pleased at every hour of the day or night without molestation, unless they had committed some violation of law for which a white man would be punished; and it would give them the full liberty of speech in public and private upon all subjects, to hold meetings upon political affairs, and to keep and carry arms wherever they went. And all of this would be done in the face of the subject race of the same color and inevitably producing discontent and insubordination among them, and endangering the peace and safety of the state."

It seems inescapable that the true content of feeling toward black people, legally and socially, has never really changed in this country. Perhaps it is only a crust, cracking and about to break asunder in this revolutionary age. We do not know how thick this crust is; we know it is cracking. We should fear that it will tremble and shake apart into a gulf of disaster which may topple whole cities into irretrievable ruin, as San Francisco was toppled and burned by a fault in the earth some years ago. There is a fault in the American earth; it is deep, it is rumbling out a warning. We should listen.

If we do not listen, if we persist in so brutally suppressing the surface demonstration, the dialogue between us and the black people will end: soon they will not talk to us any more. This is what happened, and it is still happening, in Africa, in those places where we did not begin to decolonialize in time. Jean Paul Sartre, in a warning to Europeans about the ending of this dialogue, writes [56] "After a few steps in the darkness you will see strangers gathered around a fire; come close, and listen, for they are talking of the destiny they will mete out to your trading centers and to the hired soldiers who defend them. They will see you, perhaps, but they will go on talking among themselves, without even lowering their voices . . . These constantly renewed aggressions, far from bringing them to submission, thrust them into an unbearable contradiction which the European will pay for sooner or later . . . when they are taught what hunger and shame and pain are, all that is stirred up in them is a volcanic fury whose force is equal to that of the pressure put upon them . . . Make no mistake about it; by this mad fury, by this bitterness and spleen . . . by the permanent tensing of powerful muscles which are afraid to relax, they have become men; men *because of* the settler, who wants to make beasts of burden of them— because of him and against him. Hatred, blind hatred which is as yet an abstraction, is their only wealth . . ."

In my opinion this degree of hatred for the oppressor does not yet exist in Harlem. There are still a few simple pleasures, acts of tenderness that can be carried out and which will have to be completely rooted out before a person can absolutely hate. These boys, for example, these six boys had a pigeon club on the roofs of Harlem. Ironically, they love to train homing pigeons, train them to fly away a little, and then come back to Harlem. [57]

MRS. HAMM

Danny wants to be a veterinarian;
He is very fond of pigeons and dogs.
He has to be fond of them, because
Every time I turned around in my house I had
    pigeons underfoot.
And they are still there,
Because my younger boy is taking care of the
    pigeons.
The same pigeons!

MRS. CRAIG

And Willie cared so much for them,
When it was cold like this he would bring
    them in . . .
In boxes, in big boxes, and put them in his room
And keep them there till it got warm.
The boys ask us all the time how the pigeons are.
But they tell me to tell the kids to stay off the roof
Because there's no telling what the police
Might get up there and do to them . . .
Because the pigeon coop is still up there.

MRS. HAMM

The police would rather have them down in the
    street
Than up there out of danger and out of
Doing things that's wrong.
Up on the roof they're not bothering anybody.
They're up there . . . they're having fun
Taking care of the pigeons,
Staying out of trouble.
They would take their food up there and eat.
Danny come in the morning and ask for money to
    buy his food,
Go there in the morning before they went to school.
They even went so far to build a burglar alarm
For the pigeons, because some kids would come
And steal their pigeons and sell them back to
    the people

They buy them from.
Then, when we give them their allowance,
They take that and buy pigeons.
They used to come home lots of times and say
Gosh, I'm real hungry, and I'd say
What did you do with your lunch money?
And they tell me, I bought some more pigeons.
So I give him some more money for pigeons.
If he likes that I want him to enjoy himself.

MRS. CRAIG

Willie had a special drawer in his room
That he kept the pigeon food in . . .
And the sick ones . . . sometimes you would hear
Cheep, cheep, and you look under the bed
And he would have brought in a sick pigeon . . .

Harlem is healthy; there is a profound health in these mothers and there must be some of it in their sons. Think of what they surmount there every day, and what they have to pay for their acts of goodness and decency. No bookie or racketeer was ever known to have been roughed up in these precinct houses—only those who perform a small act of resistance. In fact, it was the first small act of resistance that brought these six boys as a group to the attention of the police. [58]

MRS. HAMM

One day the kids were up on the roof with the
   pigeons
And two carloads of detectives came and went up
   on the roof.
They pulled their guns on the kids and searched
   them
And made them all come down, and they were
   going to
Take them down to the precinct.
My daughter came to my house and got me,
And I went around to Seventh Avenue to see what
   was happening.

The boys were talking amongst themselves,
And they were saying they didn't do anything
And they weren't going anywhere.
So one of the kids asked me . . .
If you will go with me I will go to the precinct.
I said no, I'll go and I'll find out what's wrong.
When I went to the precinct the cops, the
    detectives was there,
And I heard one of them say
To get those boys to the precinct we would have to
    shoot them.
There was a big crowd around them,
And the police seemed like they was embarrassed,
Because I don't think they expected the kids.
To have as much sense as they had in speaking up
    for themselves.
My nephew was there and he told me, he says
Just leave Danny alone, let him talk.
And they talked, they told the police they hadn't
    done anything,
And they wasn't getting into any police car,
And they wasn't going to any police station with
    them . . .
And they didn't.

The people in Harlem who believe in the innocence
of these boys feel that they were picked up by the police
because of the participation of three of them in the fruit
stand riot; they don't even know about the pigeon incident, which involved the six of them. The love for
pigeons has been part of the life of Harlem for genera-
tions. It is a marvelous example of the adaptability of
human nature to existing conditions. These winged
things, their feet unsoiled, their movements untrammeled
by the dirty asphalt, the dirty walls around them, going,
soaring in a flutter of lifting wings, then wheeling and
returning to the loving hands of their protectors . . .
these are the only pets, the only live objects of unques-
tioning love, which will not end up as mangled heaps

of guts on the streets of Harlem . . . only the air is safe.

But the police fear that the roofs of Harlem are becoming guerilla outposts. They fear them so much that they keep them under constant surveillance and may soon shoot at sight of any activity up there, and be prepared to move in and mop up any evidence of organized movement being carried on, however innocent. The logic of their present position demands this. As after the Nat Turner Rebellion, when the whole South was confronted with the accursed question Free us or we will kill you, they found a way of postponing it, with constant patrolling, lynching, with laws forbidding two or more black men to talk to one another, to be out at night, or be on the roads away from home at night without a pass . . . the old equivalent of the Stop and Frisk and No Knock laws. There is no other way of achieving a postponement of justice, but we always try. Henry Thoreau knew this and said, "They who are bred in the school of politics fail now and always to face the facts. Their measures are half measures and makeshifts, merely. They put off the day of settlement and meanwhile the debt accumulates among their faint resolves."

Meanwhile this debt, this wrong accumulates in this city, the city of light with its towers of buildings radiating light and richness, which offers a variety of sensation and pleasure that beggars the opulence of the dalliance of kings, which constantly talks about itself with ardor and admiration as if Harlem did not exist in the shadows of this forest of light. As if Harlem were not saturated with wall-to-wall cops and a show of repressive force unthinkable outside an occupied country.

This because we whites have become so cowed ourselves, so complacent about what exists in our own private spheres, that we dare not raise a finger to prevent our overlord-bureacrats from taking over our morality, making decisions for us that hurt people in our name, slaughtering Vietnamese, blockading Cubans, mounting counterrevolutionary attacks all over the world. We have become so cowed we think people with a resistant spirit are sick.

So we send into Harlem what we think are healers and coolers, the medical missionaries we call sociologists and psychologists to probe tortured psyches, to clean up a little, to plead with them to "adapt" to their unending misery. All we succeed in doing is infecting some of them with our own doubt and uncertainty . . . our hopelessness and fear in the face of a problem which demands a revolutionary solution rather than sociological or psychiatric treatment. We seem unable, as if under some form of paralysis, to perform some very simple acts, things a worker can do with his hands, like sending armies of plumbers to fix bad toilets, armies of rat-killers to expunge that horror . . . we have achieved the ability to kill millions of men in a flash of doom; why can't we get rid of rodents that gnaw children? Any house with firm walls, beams and underpinning can be made livable if not beautiful by the toil of human hands; all the obvious external horrors of Harlem lie within the limits of simple human capability. The streets could be kept clean; Park Avenue is. While the police are walking around there three abreast, let them push brooms; they can still use the sticks to hammer people over the head.

It is the Law that should be the healer. Simple compassionate justice, intelligent enforcement agencies contribute far more to the health of a community than its hospital. Thoreau says the law can never make man free if men do not make the law free. A law for free men guards the inviolability and thus the dignity of the community and its citizens by restraining acts of hostility against them. But what happens in a community when these acts of hostility and humiliation come from the Law itself?

Where the courts, which are supposed to act as Hospitals to heal, and not to punish those whose damaged psyches force them into unsocial acts, are themselves antisocial, sick and cruel! Where these Hospitals are places not of healing but of torture! Where diagnoses and formulas for cure are distorted, turned upside down until they are agents of punishment as crude as the rack and thumbscrew! Where mothers find their children, if sociatally sick will be made sicker, sick unto death, and if well and whole, will there be deeply infected with a societal hate from which they will never recover! Where the Doctors (i.e., Judges and Prosecuting Attorneys) act openly to kill and not to save the patient . . . who call for the killing of the patient as part of their duty! And where the locus of power for this dehumanizing debasement comes from outside the community and from persons almost universally of another race and culture!

The fact is, white America, blind America, racist America is finally beginning to see the black community as it really is. But it may be too late. In making it a community of victims, they have unwittingly forged a far more dangerous social entity . . . AN OPPRESSED PEOPLE . . . becoming more and more aware of the real tyranny under which they live . . . feeling more and more conscious of the need to cast it off. A man has no more right to be a victim than a criminal. And since he has become victimized as a People, he must seek redemption as a People.

The answer, the redemption process, lies deep in the American grain. It has been implanted as a morality, a guide to life in the hearts and minds of white Americans since 1776. But for the black people we have made this an ideology of lies. After bragging for two hundred years about our revolution, our humanism, our freedom, we have ended up with the inability to absorb twenty-two millions into this status of humanism because they are black. Time has proven that the Bill of Rights has been a Bill of White Rights, that the Constitution beginning We the People has always meant We the White People. But the words endure and it is still true, and still just, and still RIGHT that in this country a PEOPLE were made their own judges and that it is their own ultimate responsibility to secure themselves in the enjoyment of life, liberty and the pursuit of happiness and whenever government or court becomes destructive of these humanizing rights it is the duty of a PEOPLE to alter or abolish it and reorganize its powers as shall seem most likely to secure their dignity and happiness.

AUTHOR'S POSTSCRIPT

During the trial of these boys whose story I have told the mothers were taken separately to conference rooms by court-appointed attorneys and were entreated to prevail upon the boys to confess to a lesser charge which would let them off with a sentence of one-to-five years. The mothers meditated this tragic and agonizing dilemma for sleepless nights and then rejected the deal without consulting their sons.

The boys, mute, in the exacerbating presence of a defense felt by them to be neither skillful, compassionate, nor just, rose at one point collectively to announce their conviction that they could not get justice in "this white man's court."

For this small act of resistance they were sent to the insane ward of a nearby hospital to determine what kind of craziness had caused them not to plead guilty and receive a sentence of one-to-five years instead of life imprisonment. But Daniel Hamm, 18, Robert Rice, 17, Willie Craig, 17, Walter Thomas, 18, Wallace Baker, 19, and Ronald Felder, 18, chose to reject their forced confessions and heroically to uphold the confidence of their mothers and friends by enduring the verdict of life imprisonment, staking their lives on their innocence and a new trial.

As this edition goes to press, an appeal is being prepared. But the savage irony is that the appeal lawyers are the same ones whose betrayal put the boys behind bars in the first place.

The lawyers whom the boys want are entering the case *Amicus Curiae* which means they will be defending them, once removed — a situation so complicated that I cannot possibly explain it without writing another book.

TRUMAN NELSON

New York City, 1967

NOTES

1. Excerpt, *N.Y. Times*, May 29, 1964:

HARLEM: THE TENSION UNDERNEATH

*Youths Study Karate, Police Keep Watch
and People Worry*

by JUNIUS GRIFFIN

On April 17, about 75 Negro children on their way home from school overturned some cartons at a Harlem fruit and vegetable stand, and what might have been a minor incident grew into a riot.

The trouble, now known in Harlem as the Fruit Riot, set the stage for the expansion of anti-white youth gangs, some of whose members call themselves Blood Brothers. The police say that three Harlem youths under indictment for the recent murders of two white women are members of the Blood Brothers and participated in the Fruit Riot.

In the six weeks since the riot the Blood Brothers have intensified their training in karate and judo fighting methods, peaceful Harlem residents have become worried, and the Police Department has detailed some of its best men to concentrate on the central Harlem area.

An account of the events of that April day and their consequences has now been pieced together. This reporter has inquired into the story in Harlem for four weeks, talking with policemen, with participants in and witnesses of the riot, and with other members of the Harlem community who are concerned in the current uneasiness.

April 17 was a sunny Friday, and the pupils, in a holiday mood, decided to take a few apples and oranges from Joe's Fruit Stand at 368 Lenox Avenue.

When two stands were overturned, the children grabbed at the spilled fruit, Four patrolmen tried to catch the offenders, whose cries attracted to the scene some tough teen-aged members of Harlem gangs. The teen-agers jeered the patrolmen, and reenforcements were summoned.

Policemen emerged from patrol cars with pistols drawn and nightsticks swinging.

Local businessmen and passersby said that a Harlem resident who tried to stop the fracas suffered injuries that resulted in loss of an eye. According to them, some youngsters who were merely onlookers were beaten on the head. Four policemen were injured.

Several persons were arrested. Charges of police brutality were made by Harlem residents.

Police officials have denied the brutality charges, but refused to elaborate. "We will not dignify the charges," one official explained.

Whatever goodwill had existed between the police and the community turned to hostility.

The temper of central Harlem grew sullen, as residents complained about the policemen's "inept handling of a minor situation."

The self-styled Blood Brothers apparently believed they had a ready-made recruiting cry. They seized on the Fruit Riot as the means to expand their anti-white forces. The Blood Brothers were able to indoctrinate an increasing number of youths with militant anti-white sentiment.

Social workers and community leaders trace the anti-white philosophy of Harlem youth gangs to 1959, the year when the Black Muslim and Black Nationalist movements began to spread. Malcolm X, who formerly headed the Black Muslim Harlem Mosque, and who was noted for his speeches denouncing the white man, became the idol of many of Harlem's youths.

Malcolm broke away from the parent Black Muslim group last March and formed Muslim Mosque, a Black Nationalist group.

His Black Nationalist organization is one of nine such groups in Harlem advocating Black control and unity in economics, politics and social activities of the Negro, patterned on the emerging new nations of Africa.

Black-against-black gang fights have disappeared and many of Harlem's youths have found new interest in Africa and its leaders.

Within three years, about 5,000 apostate Black Muslims had fanned out in the Harlem community. They adopted Malcolm's anti-white philosophy.

TRAINED IN KARATE AND JUDO

It was the philosophy of this group that encouraged the formation of the Blood Brothers and three or four similar gangs. While there is no known connection between Malcolm X and the Blood Brothers, dissident Black Muslims have trained senior members of the gang.

The Blood Brothers appear to be distinguished from other youth gangs chiefly by their intensive training in karate and judo fighting techniques. According to members, they are organized into divisions, each division consisting of a junior and senior league. Communication among divisions is maintained by a system of runners.

Various estimates have been made of the strength of the Blood Brotherhood. First police estimates were put at about 90. Some believe there is a hard core of only 25. Other sources say there are as many as 400. A gang leader told this reporter that there were now 200 trained Blood Brothers, and that each trainee was obligated to train at least 10 juniors. Exact figures have been difficult to come by since the burgeoning movement received wide publicity a month ago. Many members have reportedly gone underground, and others have become inactive in an effort to escape interrogation by the special police corps newly assigned to Harlem.

A spokesman for the community centers operated by the Board of Education in central Harlem recently revealed that personnel of the centers had become aware of the Blood Brothers' existence in early March.

He added that their existence was hinted at as early as January, when teachers in charge of various centers reported hearing an unusual amount of anti-white sentiment.

The centers have since identified about 25 members of the Blood Brothers and an additional 25 youths who they say are "on the fringe."

The group was said to have openly recruited members in at least two of the board's 21 centers in Harlem until its operations were uncovered.

OFFSHOOT FAVORS VIOLENCE

The recruiting was said to have been done by a few (two to six) "very cool and very sick kids," who seemed to have been thoroughly indoctrinated with the hate-white theme of the Muslims.

However, a spokesman for the centers said, the recruits were "way-out half-wits" looking for kicks.

In one center, it was reported, a few youths arranged for a karate session to be taught by a Japanese. Two sessions were held before the center's supervisor learned of the sessions and stopped them. It could not be learned where the youngsters had obtained the money for the lessons.

The centers now are working closely with the police, turning over information on any youth suspected of being a Blood Brother.

Another agency, the Youth Board, operated by the city to deal with juvenile problems, said it had not uncovered the actual existence of the gang, but had had hints of it. The board said it had assigned three Negro workers to investigate the hints.

Apparently these investigators have not encountered, as this reporter has, a number of admitted members of the Blood Brotherhood.

One such member recently volunteered the information that there was in existence an off-shoot of the Brotherhood known as the Black Mollyzuls. He described this gang as a "colored organization — they wear red, black and green, and mostly they believe in violence and killing white."

"The Blood Brothers is two organizations," he said. "One believes in killing and murdering and one believes in helping and fighting back — if they be hit first, of course."

It was late last year that the Harlem police first noticed a pattern in juvenile crime in the area. Muggings and other crimes were being committed mainly against white persons. And the youthful offenders had an extensive knowledge of karate and judo.

Attention was focused on these facts last Oct. 21, when Jules Bulgach, a 71-year-old white fruit peddler, was stabbed to death on a Harlem street.

The police received a tip about the existence of an anti-white youth gang with the avowed intention of attacking white people.

The second murder of a white person occurred on March 23. David Watts, 29, who had come to Harlem from Idaho seven years ago to live as a missionary and conduct Bible studies, was slain in the street.

THEN MORE SLAYINGS

Less than a month later, on April 11, Eileen Johnson, 28, a white Department of Welfare social worker, was stabbed to death as she walked with a Negro co-worker near 150 West 131st Street.

And on April 29 came the knife slaying of Mrs. Margit Sugar in her second-hand clothing store at 3 West 125th Street, for which three alleged members of the Blood Brothers have been indicted.

The youths are Daniel Hamm, 18, of 26 West 131st Street; Wallace Baker, 19, of 2817 Seventh Avenue, and Robert Rice, 17, of 18 West 127th Street. The police say that Hamm and Rice have also admitted stabbing to death Miss Johnson.

The indicted youths were with Blood Brothers who took part in the April 17 fruit riot. They were interviewed about the riot on April 20 by Harlem Youth Unlimited (HARYOU), a community self-help organization. According to the tape-recorded interview, Hamm said they "heard a siren, a police siren, and we didn't pay too much attention to it, and we heard children scream.

"As I got closer to the corner, I saw this policeman with his gun out, waving it in some young children's faces, with his billy in his hand. I put myself in the way to keep him from shooting the kids, because, first of all, he was shaking like a leaf and jumping all over the place and I thought he might shoot one of them. So I stepped in his way to keep one of the kids from getting hurt trying to find out what was going on, and he turned on me.

"In return I tried to get out of his way but as I ran and got in the middle of the street, a patrolman apprehended me by the neck, flipped me over and put his knee in my chest . . .

"He handcuffed me, and I was handcuffed in front, and he took me to the patrol car and later on one of my friends that was with me named Wallace Baker . . . he put him in the car, too.

POLICE DENY BEATINGS

"We went to the precinct and that's where they beat us, like 12 and 6 at a time would beat us and this went on practically all that day when we were in the station. Fortunately, when they threw us on the floor, I was fortunate enough to crawl under the bench so I wouldn't get whipped so bad. They beat me till I couldn't barely walk and my back was in pain.

"My friends they did the same till they bled, but I was the only . . . oh, I'm so mixed up now, that's all I have to say for now."

Baker and Rice gave similar testimony. Baker, however, admitted that he resisted arrest and struck back at a policeman.

The police have categorically denied the beatings.

Baker and Hamm have been charged with felonious assault in connection with the fruit riot.

Another Blood Brother who was at the scene of the fruit riot said that after the youngsters were taken to the police station a woman known as Yolanda X of 145 West 130th Street, whose husband is an apostate Black Muslim, led 30 Blood Brothers to the station, but the police ringed the station and they could not get in.

The background and sentiments of the Blood Brothers are typified by one 17-year-old who lives with his younger brother, three sisters and mother on the third floor of a central Harlem tenement.

"Why shouldn't I be a Blood Brother? . . . Why shouldn't I hate all white people?" he asked during an interview.

HAD TO GET MONEY

The youth, unemployed, and seeking a job for the last year, said he had joined the Blood Brothers almost six months ago when his mother became ill and could not work.

"I had to make a 'hit' (get some money)," he said. "Some of my friends said that if I needed rent money that they knew a group who would help. We stole $58 from a store where I used to work. There was more, but we only took what I needed to pay the rent."

Each night before going to bed, he spends half an hour jabbing his hands into a pail of gravel. This is standard practice among Blood Brothers — designed to toughen the hands.

Rice is preferred, but the rice he had bought was cooked by his sister when the family food supply dwindled.

The youth shares a bedroom with his younger brother and adolescent sister, who finds the arrangement embarrassing. In the Blood Brotherhood, the youth finds an escape from the sordidness and depression of his life. He is looking forward to a planned "hit," or attack, against Harlem police, probably sometime in July, to protest the enforcement of the "no-knock" and "stop-and-frisk" laws, which become effective July 1.

These state laws, which gang members view as being

directed mainly against Harlem, would permit the police to enter homes, search and seize persons without warrants.

The exact date of the "hit," according to one gang leader, will be decided within 48 hours of the attack in order to lessen chances of betrayal.

HATRED FOR THE POLICE

The Blood Brothers freely admit a hatred of precinct patrolmen, but express an even more intense hatred of the Tactical Patrol Force officers who have been sent into central Harlem since the fruit riot.

In central Harlem it is not unusual to see as many as four members of the Judo-trained Tactical Patrol Force deployed on a single street corner.

One Negro precinct officer, who asked not to be identified, explained: "We'd rather not have the T.P.F.'s in the area. First, they don't know these people as we do, and whereas we might settle a street dispute by sending both parties on their separate ways, they are apt to explode community tensions by their very direct application of the letter of the law."

While the Police Department considers the new anti-white gangs in Harlem a major problem and has undertaken a major effort to combat them, *Commissioner Michael J. Murphy will not publicly acknowledge the existence of the gangs.*

It has been learned from other sources, however, that Commissioner Murphy has been getting periodic reports from Assistant Chief Inspector Joseph L. Coyle, the commander of the Manhattan North Detective Division which includes Harlem.

The effort to hold the gangs in check is centered in the 32nd Detective Squad, whose headquarters are at 250 West 135th Street.

Lieut. Arthur E. Young, the squad's commanding officer, is in charge of the detective work.

This squad's efforts are being supplemented by a special detail of undercover men working out of the Central Investigation Bureau. The group is composed of hand-picked Negro detectives. Its size is not known, even to most of the detectives and patrolmen regularly assigned to the area.

The 50 members of the Tactical Patrol Force who have been assigned to the 32nd Precinct arrive late every afternoon — most of them in a departmental bus — and work on the night shift.

Their function, as one detective put it, is "to lower the temperature of this place, to keep it from reaching the boiling point."

Working in pairs, the tactical patrolmen are able to saturate the area (Commissioner Murphy calls them "wall-to-wall cops"). They are said to be arresting, on various charges, scores of persons whom the regular patrolmen — swamped with work in a high-crime area — would have to overlook.

All members of the special force are at least six feet tall. In addition to training in judo, they are instructed in what the department calls "human relations." They attempt to put into effect what Mr. Murphy sometimes calls his philosophy of police work: the substitution of a show of force for the actual use of force.

Even without these reinforcements the 32nd Precinct is one of the most heavily policed areas in the city.

Patrolmen and detectives, as elsewhere in the city, are assigned without regard to race. As a result, Negroes are in the minority.

POLICE TAKE PRECAUTIONS

It is known that the police approached the directors of Board of Education community centers in the area in March, seeking information about members of Blood Brotherhood.

Detectives are also working with a number of informers, several of whom are said to be close to members of the gang and to have provided valuable information. From these and other sources, the police have built substantial dossiers on "known" and "suspected" members.

In an effort to avoid trouble, many policemen in the area have taken extraordinary precautions. A white detective told a reporter recently that he no longer frisked suspects on the street, as he once did, but took them into doorways.

"Almost anything like this can set off a small riot these days," he explained.

An increase — or, at least a continuation — of the Harlem community's ill will toward the police in recent weeks is generally acknowledged. The phrase "police brutality" is repeated like a litany by Harlem residents of all ages and economic levels.

Commissioner Murphy has repeatedly denied that any pattern of brutality exists, although he has conceded that isolated cases do occur. In an attempt to reduce friction, he and his aides have undertaken a public relations campaign designed to win over the Negro leadership.

PSYCHOLOGICAL WAR ON STREETS

But the Negro community decries the concentration of policemen in Harlem. The Police Department, on the other hand, asserts the community is indifferent to the rising tide of violence and to a militant youth movement.

Most of Harlem's middle-class Negroes deny the existence of the anti-white youth gangs, but they admit that conditions in the community could very well spur such a group. They say that the Blood Brotherhood is a "myth" created by the police and the white press to smear Harlem.

Policemen who walk their beats in central Harlem are subject to an unusual kind of psychological warfare.

At 8 P.M. on May 14, for example, two white policemen turned right off Seventh Avenue into 129th Street. A youngster sprinted up the opposite side of the street ahead of the police, warning others that "the rollers" (police) were coming.

Half way up the block just in front of the policemen, a bottle crashed on the sidewalk, thrown from the roof of a tenement.

The patrolmen, in their 20's, tensed and flushed, looked up, and then tried to appear unperturbed. They strolled on, one with his nightstick in his right hand, the other with his stick swinging by a leather sling from his badge.

As they passed several stoops, they were denounced by youths and adults. Some called them "dirty cops," "white bastards" and "no good killers."

The patrolmen looked ahead walking shoulder to shoulder with almost military precision.

Four teen-agers playing a card game called "tonk" gathered their cards from the stoop as the patrolmen approached. The patrolmen pretended not to notice. The end of the block was near.

Slowly they turned onto Lenox Avenue, leaned against a building and mopped their brows.

"We made it," said one of them.

A patrol car pulled up to the curb and the two men conversed briefly with its occupant, a police sergeant.

When the car moved away, the two patrolmen stood on the corner, chatting. A group of Negro youngsters came toward them from across the street.

The two policemen talked to the children for a few minutes.

One of the policemen patted a child on the head, then walked off.

Six Blood Brothers had watched the scene, two from a roof, the others, from the block. Two 10-year-old boys used as runners had stood by to spread the word to other blocks, just in case the "rollers" had made "a bad move."

In an interview, a Blood Brothers leader said that "the main reason the gang started was to protect ourselves in a group against police brutality."

"If they're going to hit one of us, and we're by ourselves, then there's no protection," he said, "but if there's a group of us fighting against the police we have a better chance of — you know — getting out of it."

The gang leader said that he and his fellow members relied on karate and judo, because "with a gun in your pocket, or knife, or anything else — you can always lose that — but you never drop your hands or leave your hands at home."

The gang leader is training a group of 17 juniors living in his block. His methods and the respect he commands from his 10-to-15-year-olds are not unlike those of a Marine Corps drill instructor.

WHAT GROUP IS TAUGHT

No attempt is made to indoctrinate the juniors in any religious or hate philosophies. They are taught, rather, not to be afraid of policemen, and how to defend themselves in a fight with "Whitey" or with Puerto Ricans. "Whitey" has become a term of contempt used by many Negroes for the white man.

On the second floor of a vacant building this reporter recently watched the leader put his charges through their paces.

They formed a single line in front of the gang leader. He commanded:

"Karate stance . . . move."

Seventeen young bodies snapped into a position with the left foot and left hand extended and the right hand and right foot braced. Knuckles were turned toward the floor.

They went through karate rolls, holds, throws and hand-toughening exercises. The leader sent for a thin wooden board. Each youngster was given a turn at trying to break the board with the edge of his hand. After all had failed, the leader crushed the board with a single right-hand blow.

Another board was set up and various members of the group attempted to break it with a karate kick. A 10-year-old broke the board and earned the price of a soda.

The session was over and the gang leader announced the meeting place for the next night.

Walking out of the building, one of the youngsters said proudly, "I bet I could take that cop's gun."

The gang leader, an unusually articulate youth, said that he attributed the anti-white feeling among his group to "police brutality" because the majority of the Harlem policemen were white.

Asked if he had trouble with Negro policemen, he replied: "Well, there are Negro policemen who do this, but I take this as them doing this in the line of duty. Some of them are scared that maybe a teen-ager does have a weapon on him."

Commenting on the three youths who are charged with the murder of two white persons, the Blood Brother leader said: "You'd be surprised how a teen-ager's feelings can be twisted around by brutality acts and wounds inflicted on them.

A MATTER OF REVENGE

"Maybe these boys had things done to them by white policemen, or maybe some other white person has done something to them and he can't get back at that person. Well, then, again he'll take it out on anybody he sees."

The youth refused to say whether there was any connection between the Blood Brothers and the Black Muslims, but he tried to explain his own anti-white feelings.

"As far as I know, every white person I've met has been against Negroes," he said. "And that's, I think, the same with the majority of the Blood Brothers."

The youngster said that he believed there was at least one organization in Harlem able to establish some type of communication with the Blood Brothers and probably help them in trying to find jobs.

He said that he thought that organization was the United

Block Association, whose leaders and volunteer workers live and work in their neighborhoods.

The Block Association, which is headed by Earl Lewis and Billy Rolle, was evicted on May 10 from its headquarters at 170 West 130th Street for failing to pay its rent.

2. Excerpt, *N.Y. Times*, April 19, 1964:

LAWYER FOR 5 TELLS COURT
POLICE ROUGHED UP CLIENTS

A lawyer representing five defendants charged with Sullivan Law Violations, felonious assault and malicious mischief accused the police of brutality yesterday in Criminal Court.

The lawyer, George Senna, was told by Judge Maurice W. Corey to take his complaint to Police Commissioner Michael J. Murphy.

The defendants, four youths and a man, were involved in a free-for-all on Friday afternoon after they allegedly overturned a fruit stand at 368 Lenox Avenue, near 128th St. Four of the defendants appeared in court wearing bandages, and the fifth was in Bellevue Hospital for an eye injury. Four patrolmen who were injured were treated at Harlem Hospital for cuts and bruises.

The defendants were held in bail ranging from $500 to $1,000 and the case was adjourned to Thursday.

3. Tape made by interviewer Willie Jones for Harlem Youth Unlimited, known as HARYOU.
4. Ibid.
5. Tape made by Truman Nelson
6. Haryou Tape
7. Nelson Tape
8. Haryou Tape
9. Ibid.
10. Ibid.
11. Ibid.
12. Nelson Tape
13. Ibid.
14. Ibid.
15. Ibid.
16. Excerpt, *N.Y. Times*, January 13, 1965:

POLICE LIEUTENANT IS GUILTY
OF SELLING BOGUS $20 BILLS

Police Lieut. Vincent Satriano, suspended from the force, pleaded guilty yesterday in Brooklyn Federal Court to conspiring to sell counterfeit $20 bills.

He faces a possible five-year prison term when he is sentenced Feb. 26.

An all-male jury had been chosen Tuesday, and trial was about to begin when Lieutenant Satriano entered a guilty plea through his lawyer, Arthur Lubell. Judge Walter Bruchhausen accepted the plea.

The 39-year-old police officer, who has earned 32 citations for bravery and outstanding performance of duty in 17 years with the department, was arrested Nov. 30. He was accused of selling 50 bogus $20 bills for about $150 to Joseph T. DeVesta, a Brooklyn automobile salesman. DeVesta was named as a co-conspirator but not indicted.

17. Tape made by Willie Jones independently
18. Nelson Tape
19. Jones Tape
20. Excerpt, *N.Y. Times*, May 5, 1964:

SUSPECT GIVES UP IN HARLEM DEATH

Negro Youth Is 3rd Accused in Shopkeeper's Murder

A 19-year-old Negro suspect in the slaying of a white shopkeeper surrendered yesterday to the police on a Harlem street and was charged with homicide.

The police are investigating the possibility that he was a member of a gang of about 60 young Negroes who, after being trained to maim and kill, roam the streets of Harlem attacking white people.

The suspect was identified as Wallace Baker, of 2187 Seventh Avenue. He was the third Negro teen-ager charged with homicide in the slaying last Wednesday of Mrs. Margit Sugar, 45, and the wounding of her husband, Frank, 50, in the couple's second-hand clothing store at 3 West 125th Street. Three other youths have been charged with felonious assault in the case. The police said that by pre-arrangement, Baker, accompanied by his lawyer, George Senna, surrendered to three detectives at 8:45 A.M. at Broadway and 100th Street.

The police had issued an alarm for Baker last Friday. At that time they said that they believed Baker had actually been the one who stabbed Mrs. Sugar in the heart.

Baker was also charged with felonious assault in the stabbing of Mrs. Sugar. He, along with the other five teen-agers, are being questioned in several other Harlem murders involving white victims.

Yesterday's edition of *El Diario La Prensa*, a Spanish-language newspaper often critical of police dealings with Puerto-Ricans and Negroes, carried an editorial in which it said "it is horrifying to learn that the action (the killing of Mrs. Sugar) is suspected to have been a premeditated attack by a band of Negroes on whites solely for the reason of race."

"Our place is with the forces of law and order and not with violence and disorder," the editorial said.

It said that in cases of violence "the police must inevitably intervene."

"We predict that there will be a hue and cry of 'police brutality' on the heels of these incidents. But it will not be in *El Diario La Prensa*," the editorial said.

21. Ibid.
22. Excerpt, *N.Y. Times*, May 1, 1964:

3 YOUTHS SEIZED IN HARLEM KILLING

A Racial Motive in Recent Assaults Is Investigated

Three youths were arrested yesterday in connection with the fatal stabbing of a Harlem shopkeeper and the wounding of her husband on Wednesday.

A detective disclosed that the attack might have been the latest in a series of incidents in which militant and organized bands of Negro toughs have assaulted whites with seemingly no motive.

The detective, who is attached to the West 123d Street station house, said that police were investigating a number of recent killings and assaults in Harlem that seemed to be the work of racists.

Asked whether this last killing fit into this pattern, the detective, who asked that he not be identified, replied, "I can't say yes and I can't say no — it's possible."

The victims of Wednesday's attack were Margit Sugar, 50 years old, and her husband Frank, 47, who operated a second-hand clothing store at 3 West 125th Street.

Mr. Sugar, who is in fair condition at Physicians' Hospital in Jackson Heights, Queens, gave police this account of the incident:

A group of boys entered the store just before 5 P.M. They took up positions around the shop and began taunting the proprietors.

When one of the youths asked to see a suit, Mrs. Sugar replied that they had none in his size. Another youth then drew a knife and stabbed the woman once in the heart.

Mr. Sugar was slashed and stabbed several times when he grappled with the knife wielder.

Julius Levitt, who operates a drugstore next door, heard the commotion and sent his delivery boy to see what was happening. After his employee had reported back and the druggist had seen the group run out of the clothing store he called the police.

Yesterday morning the police arrested the three suspects. They were arraigned before Judge Samuel J. Ohringer on charges of felonious assault and violation of the weapons law. The police were still seeking four others.

A homicide charge was held open until it could be determined which boy did the killing.

Those arrested were Ronald Felder of 159 West 129th Street and Walter Thomas of 163 West 129th Street, both 18 years old, and Willie Craig of 2183 Seventh Avenue, 17.

The detective at the 123d Street precinct said that while the three youths had denied being members of the Black Muslims, a police informant has definitely identified them as belonging to the Muslim group.

The detective said that it was the knowledge of the youths' link with the Muslims that had led to their speedy arrests. He said that during the last few months, detectives of the 28th and 32d precincts had been investigating possible ties between militant groups and a number of assaults.

Henry X, a spokesman for the New York Mosque of the Black Muslim movement said in response to a question that his group "does not advocate stuff like that."

The police have recovered the murder weapon. It was a six-inch English made dirk with a double edge, tapered to a point.

23. Excerpt, *Daily News*, May 26, 1964 (*the only report not mentioning the "racial" implications of the murder*):

INDICT 6 TEENS IN KNIFE DEATH

Six teen-agers were indicted on first degree murder charges yesterday in the knife slaying April 29 of Mrs. Margit Sugar, 45, in her second-hand clothing store at 3 W. 125th St.

They were also indicted for attempted robbery and attempted murder in the stabbing of her husband, Frank, 50.

The youths were Daniel Hamm, 18, of 26 W. 131st St.; Robert Rice, 17, of 18 W. 127th St.; Wallace Baker, 19, of 2187 Seventh Ave.; Ronald Felder, 18, of 163 W. 129th St.; and William Craig, 17, of 2183 Seventh Ave.

Police said that Hamm and Rice admitted stabbing to death Eileen Johnson, 28, a Welfare Department social worker, on a Harlem street April 11.

While the excerpt from the *N.Y. Herald Tribune*, May 26, 1964, repeats verbatim the police version of the murder:

6 YOUTHS INDICTED IN KILLING OF WOMAN

The six Negro youths accused of walking into Mrs. Margit Sugar's Harlem second-hand clothing store April 29, stabbing the 45-year-old woman to death and critically wounding her husband Frank were indicted yesterday on first-degree murder charges.

All six also indicted on attempted first-degree murder charges in the stabbing of Mr. Sugar, 50, a Hungarian refugee who came to this country with his wife in 1957, following the anti-Communist uprising.

Police have said two of the youths indicted, Daniel Hamm, 18, of 26 W. 131st St., and Robert Rice, 17, of 18 W. 127th St., have also admitted stabbing to death Miss Eileen Johnson, 28, a white Department of Welfare social worker, last April 11.

All six youths have been identified as members of the "Blood Brothers" anti-white gang said to be operating in Harlem. Negro leaders deny knowledge of the existence of such a gang.

Indicted with Rice and Hamm yesterday were Wallace Baker, 19, of 2187 7th Ave.; Walter Thomas, 18, of 164 W. 129th St.; William Craig, 17, of 2183 7th Ave., and Ronald Felder, 18, of 159 W. 129th St.

Baker was said by police to be the actual killer of Mrs. Sugar. Previous to the killing, on April 17, he and Hamm were charged with felonious assault in a free-for-all between some 75 Negroes and police on a Harlem sidewalk.

In the Sugar killing, a group of young Negroes entered the couple's store at 3 W. 125th St. and two asked to see suits. Mrs. Sugar apparently was frightened and said she did not have the proper sizes. One of the youths stabbed her with a dirk, and when Mr. Sugar ran to his wife's aid, he, too, was stabbed.

The indictments were filed before Supreme Court Justice Gerald P. Culkin, who put over the arraignment of the six until June 3.

Justice Culkin ordered the delay to give the youths time to decide whether to choose their own counsels or accept court-appointed attorneys.

Excerpt, *N.Y. Times,* May 26, 1964 (*the most specifically racist: "The defendants are all Negroes; the victims of the knifing were white."*):

6 YOUTHS INDICTED IN HARLEM SLAYING

Six youths were indicted yesterday for first-degree murder in the April 29 slaying of Mrs. Margit Sugar in her clothing store in Harlem. The defendants, 17 to 19 years old, were also charged with the attempted murder of Mrs. Sugar's husband, Frank, and with attempted robbery.

Supreme Court Justice Gerald P. Culkin adjourned to June 3 the arraignment of the six because legal counsel has not yet been named for the defendants.

The defendants are all Negroes; the victims of the knifings were white. Since Mrs. Sugar was killed, there have been reports that there is a group of young Negroes whose aim is to kill or maim white persons.

Morris Levy, a lawyer who represented one of the defendants after his arrest, said yesterday outside court that he had heard "reports and rumors" of an anti-white gang but that his client, Ronald Felder, 18, of 159 West 129th Street, had told him that he did not belong to any such gang.

The defendants, in addition to Felder, are Daniel Hamm, 18, of 26 West 131st Street; Robert Rice, 17, of 18 West 127th Street; Wallace Baker, 19, of 2187 Seventh Avenue;

Walter Thomas, 18, of 163 West 129th Street, and William Craig, 17, of 2183 Seventh Avenue.

24. See Note 1.
25. Willie Jones Tape
26. See Note 1.
27. Ibid.
28. See Note 22
29. Haryou Tape
30. Ibid.
31. Ibid.
32. Ibid.
33. Ibid.
34. Ibid.
35. Ibid.
36. Ibid.
37. Oedipus Rex
38. See Note 1
39. Nelson Tape
40. Nelson Tape
41. Ibid.
42. Ibid.
43. Willie Jones Tape
44. Nelson Tape
45. Ibid.
46. Ibid.
47. Ibid.
48. *People vs. Fuller*, Court of General Sessions, May, 1901
49. See *100 Years of Lynchings*, Ginzburg, pp. 30–44
50. *Report of Select Committee on Senate on Harper's Ferry Invasion*, 1860, p. 154
51. New York Times, May 11, 1964
52. Nelson Tape
53. New York Times, August 8, 1964
54. Dred Scott Decision, March 6, 1857
55. Ibid.
56. Introduction to *The Damned* by Franz Fanon, Paris, 1963
57. Nelson Tape
58. Nelson Tape